ALSO BY SANDY LINVER

Speak Easy

Speak and Get Results

THE

LEADER'S EDGE

How to Use Communication to Grow Your
Business and Yourself

SANDY LINVER

with Jim Mengert

SIMON & SCHUSTER
NEW YORK   LONDON   TORONTO   SYDNEY   TOKYO   SINGAPORE

SIMON & SCHUSTER
Rockefeller Center
1230 Avenue of the Americas
New York, New York 10020

DESIGNED BY BARBARA MARKS

Manufactured in the United States of America

1   3   5   7   9   10   8   6   4   2

Library of Congress Cataloging-in-Publication Data
Linver, Sandy.
The leader's edge : how to use communication to
grow your business and yourself / Sandy Linver with
Jim Mengert.
p.   cm.
1. Business communication.   2. Oral
communication.   3. Public speaking.   I. Mengert,
Jim.   II. Title.
HF5718.L558   1994
858.4'5—dc20   94-1692
CIP
ISBN: 0-671-88179-5

ACKNOWLEDGMENTS

Special thanks to:

Wendy Nicholson of Simon & Schuster, who has her own experience of the journey, and has made each of my books better through her advice and encouragement. And my editors, Dominick Anfuso and Cassie Jones, who helped make this book a reality.

Bernhard Kempler, who has been an important part of Speakeasy's journey.

All of Speakeasy's clients and staff, who believe that "good enough isn't."

This book is for those special people who have supported me in my journey.

Buddy, my life partner, whose love always gives me more courage for the next step.

Jean Harsch, who helped me love my wild child and, as a result, become even more of who I wanted to be.

Neal Eldridge, who reminded me that the wand was in my own hand.

CONTENTS

TO THE READER

Have you ever been in a communication situation and wished you could be getting more out of it—more response from others, more satisfaction for yourself? Maybe it's a meeting with the executive committee, a talk to security analysts, or a performance evaluation with a direct report. It's going well enough, but something inside you knows that more is possible, and you want it.

It's not that you haven't worked on your communication during your career—read some books, listened to presentations on the subject, even attended a workshop or two. You've learned something from all of these, and would probably describe yourself as a pretty good communicator. But that's not good enough for you. You want more.

You want more because you're a leader at some level of your organization. You know that communication is one of a leader's key responsibilities, and that effective communication is one of his most valuable tools.

If this describes you, then you're the reader I've written this book for. I wanted to share with you the insights I've gained from working with business leaders on their communication for over two decades. And to introduce you to people who, at some point in their careers, began to treat communication not as a collection of separate or isolated skills, but as a long-term development process—a journey that has brought them both professional success and personal satisfaction.

The leaders you'll meet in this book are all in very different places with their own journey. Some are just beginning, and others have been working on their communication for almost twenty years. Some are already very effective, others less so. But they're all committed to moving forward. I'm offering them to you, not as models to imitate, but as examples to learn from and, perhaps, be inspired by.

You'll get to know them as you read through this book. You'll also notice that, although several of the hundreds of companies Speakeasy works with are represented here, executives from three in particular appear more frequently: The Coca-Cola Company, Andersen Consulting, and Arthur Andersen. The reason for this is that these companies were among my first clients. Since the communication journey is a life journey, I went to people who have worked with me over the longest period of time and who are in companies whose leadership, I believe, has an unusual commitment to excellence in communication. I thought that the experiences of these executives especially would give you a fuller picture of the journey.

When I asked people to be a part of this book, I was really pleased. They all accepted and were amazingly open in sharing their process. The risks they took in talking about themselves gave me more courage to share my own values and beliefs with you. This is a better book because of their part in it.

CHAPTER ONE

LOOKING BACK

SOMETHING very special happened to me last year in Hawaii. I was sitting in an audience of 2,000 people at a Coca-Cola meeting, listening to four executives whom I'd worked with and coached over many years.

As I listened, I suddenly found myself experiencing the meeting on more than one level. Having worked with most of the speakers for this meeting I knew what they were going to say and I was confident that they would do well. So I found myself looking back, imaging in my mind where each of them was years ago, when they started working on their communication. And I was feeling a lot of pleasure and satisfaction comparing that old image against the image of what they were, that day, on that stage.

Charlie Frenette, head of the Fountain division, was speaking. The image I remembered of the old Charlie was reading from a manuscript speech with an energetic delivery that came at his listeners like a machine gun. The Charlie in Hawaii was sharing with his listeners in a new way, opening up and using his wonderful energy to pull them in rather than to overwhelm them.

Amy White, vice president of Coca-Cola USA, was also on the stage that day. I remembered back to the nervous, insecure paralegal who took the Speakeasy evening class in 1977. Amy had worked hard over the years to be comfortable and technically correct, and that day was pushing beyond her previous goal of the perfect "performance"—really seeing her listeners and letting them see her passion for learning.

And Doug Ivester, then the newly appointed president of Coca-Cola USA, was having a new experience as a speaker. He was talking more about himself, not the numbers he used to talk about when he was CFO of the company, and getting reactions from his listeners. Suddenly, even with so large a group, Doug found himself having an interactive conversation, not giving a "presentation." He was connecting in a way he hadn't before with such a large group.

John Hunter, an Australian recently brought in from Japan to head up Coke's international business, was looking looser and sounding less formal than when he'd first started working on his speaking. He even mentioned his Australian heritage in a real, direct, fun way—and got a warm response from the group.

I sat in that audience feeling a deep sense of pride and pleasure for each of the people on that stage, because I knew how far they had come. And, just as important, I also knew that they were each taking a step forward that very day. Above and beyond their business goals, they were using the meeting as an opportunity to continue to explore what was possible for them as communicators. So it was not only the two images that moved me as I sat in that audience—images of speakers past and speakers present—but also the image of the speakers they still wanted to be.

These different images, of past, present, and future, floated in my mind, and helped me bring together some ideas I'd been struggling with. The sequence of images pictured for me the process that these people had been going through, their progress and growth over an extended period of time. And I saw their work on communication not as the acquisition of some specific skills but as a journey, a journey that had helped them explore and express more of themselves, both as business people and as human beings.

This idea of a communication journey is one that I have come very much to believe in. Since communication is such a complex activity, involving so many aspects of ourselves, there's always something more to learn about it. You don't become an expert in it just by taking a course or reading a book. You can always go deeper with it in some way. A lot of people don't want to hear this, because we live in a society where almost everything has been turned into a commodity, including communication training. Whether it's presentation skills or negotiating skills or listening skills, it's all packaged for quick and easy learning.

There are certainly some basic skills you can learn in a relatively short time, skills that will make you a more comfortable, more effective speaker. But to explore fully what's possible for yourself as a communicator is more than the work of a day or a week or a month. It can be a journey of years. The kind of journey those speakers at the Coke meeting had chosen to take.

None of these people began to work on their communication with the idea that they were starting on a long-term journey. They started, as most people do, because they faced a very specific problem, usually a speaking situation that was different from or more important than the ones they had been facing. Their goal at first was simply to succeed in—or survive—that situation. They were looking for ways to build their confidence and some tips from a professional to make it look easy.

At some point, however, as we worked together, they got a glimpse of the possibilities: the possibility of having an impact on others beyond what they had thought possible; of walking into a room and changing, by their presence, what happens there; the possibility of expressing their thoughts and feelings more openly, more freely, than they had allowed themselves before; of reaching out and really connecting with others. They began to want these possibilities for themselves. That's when their journey really started. And they saw me as someone who could help them on it.

If I had to summarize or condense into a single idea all the possibilities that most of my clients are trying to realize through their communication development, it would be the idea of connection. More and deeper connection with self and others is the ultimate goal of their communication journey. To me, that's not only what speaking is all about, it's what life is all about—continuing to work for a deeper connection with and understanding of yourself, taking the risk of sharing that self, and through this sharing developing a deeper and deeper connection with others.

In my work with clients, I always start with the speaker before the listener, the individual before the team. Because I believe that before you can have truly effective communication with others, you've got to be able to communicate with yourself. Connection with self is the essential first step, because you can't have an authentic connection with others if you're not in touch with yourself, with your gut as well as your head, with your body as well as your mind. I also think that getting connected with yourself is more important, and harder, today than ever before.

So many people today are struggling to adjust to enormous change in almost every area of their lives. In business, particularly, the insistent message is that we must change to survive—in an information age, in a global marketplace, in a more diverse workforce. So we're constantly upgrading our skills, adjusting our attitudes, and revising our expectations. Various "change agents" are busily working to "empower" us, sensitize us, organize us into teams, align us with the vision, focus us on our customer, and redefine our business.

In an environment where so much is changing outside us and so many people are telling us what and how to be, it's very hard for individuals to get and stay connected to themselves. It's hard for them, first of all, to get in touch with their own feelings, with what they actually think, want, and believe, and then to find the courage to express it. Yet I believe those who do this experience more personal fulfillment and professional success.

Executives who are connected with themselves and whose communication is consistent with who they are and what they want to be don't listen to the gurus. They learn to listen to themselves. They don't exhaust their energy trying to be what others tell them they need to be, but tap into the energy inside themselves. Charlie Frenette's journey has led him to this conclusion:

> *I can't change myself to meet somebody else's vision of what I should be if it's inconsistent with my own. I find that there's a lot less tension inside me when I express myself in terms of who I am as opposed to what others might want me to be. It's easier to get feedback, it's easier to learn when I'm working from a model of what I want to be as opposed to what I'm trying to be to make someone else happy.*

In other words, everything is easier for Charlie if he's connected to himself. But in my experience with different companies over many years, this self-connection is relatively rare. And even when someone is connected to himself and knows what truly energizes him, he's often unwilling to share that, to let it out. Instead, he suppresses himself, and especially his passion or energy. This happens to people at every management level, usually because they're afraid of the consequences of their own power and energy. I often see senior executives, with responsible jobs and considerable achievements, project an image that is totally incongruent with who they are. They hold back on their presence and their power because they've gotten feedback that they come on too strong or are too arrogant or aggressive. So they lose connection with their own energy core, with what motivates them and excites them, while they try to figure out who and how they're supposed to be.

Don Keough, the former president of The Coca-Cola Company and one of the most effective communicators I've ever known, is one person who decided early in his career never to suppress or hold back who he is, but to bring all his energy and passion to his work. He concedes, however, that this is rather rare:

> *What's fascinated me is how careful many business executives are at every level in opening their own person. As a result, they reach a dead end (early for some and later for others) simply because they haven't confronted the issue of saying, "I am who I am and I'm going to let people know that. When they communicate with me they will see the real me. I'm holding nothing back."*

That was exactly what was exciting me about those speakers in Hawaii—they were bringing more of themselves out, sharing more of who they were and what they believed with their listeners. Their journey had taken them beyond the facade, beyond the role, beyond even the techniques. They were more connected to themselves and willing to share that self with others. As a result, they not only experienced greater personal satisfaction, but also got the business results they wanted.

I do believe that communication has to leave room for the other person, but you don't create that space by holding back on your own passion or power. The challenge is not to deny or suppress passion, but to tap into it and then to find healthy ways to use it, ways that free you to be more of what you are and that also allow others to participate and respond. I think that one of the reasons executives choose to work with me, either in workshops or private coaching, is that I'm not afraid of their energy. I often start by asking some very simple questions, like, "What excites you?" "What would make you feel that it was worth all the effort?" "What would give you pleasure and really make you feel proud?" I want to help them tap into their energy and not worry about its impact on me. Because I believe that by getting in touch with the source of their own energy they'll be more effective communicators and leaders.

As I've said, I believe that the more connected you are to yourself, the more in touch you are with all of you, the better able you are to connect with others. This connection with others is also part of the goal of the journey. We all want to be seen and acknowledged. We want to feel that, at a given moment in time, someone else truly sees us. The person need not necessarily agree with us or like everything we say. Connection happens in those rare moments when each person feels seen by the other, when each person shares, however briefly, the other person's reality.

A lot of what I've been saying about connection may sound a bit "touchy-feely," but I actually believe there's a very practical payoff for the communicator who's always working to go deeper with connection, both with herself and others. There's power in connection, just as there is when you close an electrical circuit. Connection gives you the energy you need to respond to the challenges of business today and to involve others in the process. The executives I've worked with understand this. And I'm going to let them speak for themselves.

Frank Cella, the president of Nestlé Canada, is very clear on the business value of connecting with himself and bringing all of that self to his work.

I'm in communication situations today that have never been more challenging for me in thirty years with Nestlé, because we're not dealing with fine-tuning, but with change that's so major that it will significantly affect the future of the company. Well, that means that every decision, every talk, every report to employees becomes a monumental thing, not just something routinely done. So as I stand in front of employees today or sit one-on-one with my director of boards or whoever, I'm more conscious than ever that the whole me

*has to come out—the whole me and my opin-
ion about what's right for the company.*

Likewise, Larry Weinbach, the chief executive officer
and worldwide managing partner of Arthur Andersen
& Co, SC, understands how vital connection with others is to the firm's success:

> *If you look at how you sell your message
> within an organization, you do it through per-
> sonal communication. If I look at how I sell
> myself in dealing with clients, it's personal
> communication. It's making that personal
> connection. People form judgments quickly.
> So if you think about meeting a client or a
> prospective client, the most important thing
> to establish, up front, is some connection.*

At Speakeasy we deal with many clients from very
large companies who have access to sophisticated
technology, audiovisual support, and a lot of complex
information to help them market their companies
and their products. But my work on numerous
"pitch" presentations with clients has only confirmed
my own belief and what Larry says above—nothing
sells like the connection, like hooking into your listeners and showing them that you see them in an open,
honest way. It isn't a matter of just standing up and
rolling off a lot of polished content in a very professional way. If you have five firms all pitching for the
same piece of business, what's going to make the difference in the buyers' decision is whether or not they
feel they could work with you, that you see their

needs and understand their world. Those are chemistry reactions among people. Each person is asking himself or herself, "Do I feel a connection here? Can I trust it?"

And it's not only in external communication that the connection is critical for success. It's every bit as important internally, as Jack Stahl, the CFO of The Coca-Cola Company, fully understands:

> *What people really want from you is some sense of connection. They like the feel of it when they see it from somebody, and latch onto it. Ultimately, that's what leadership's all about. A leader has a lot of people connected to him.*
>
> *In my experience in an organization, people will change, do something differently for only two reasons: one is the personal connection. "I'll do it for him because of the connection I feel with him." The other reason is because they understand the consequences and the benefits to them. They're both important. As a leader you've got to establish the vision and what can come of that vision, but to help people move toward it, you've got to establish a connection with them.*

I know that a great deal of the joy I get in my work with clients comes not only from the satisfaction of helping them get a result, but from the connection I have working together with other human beings on things that are important to them.

I think I'll let Don Keough have the last word on the business value of connection. "I have come to the conclusion, after having been in a lot of business environments and after a long career, that there is no substitute for clear, open connection between the senior management of an organization and the people who are a part of it. It is staggering how powerful good communication can be."

EXPLORING ALL the possibilities in connection, both within yourself and with others, is, as I've said, a long-term process. But there are many rewards and successes along the way. Certainly those executives in Hawaii were experiencing some of those rewards at that meeting. Each had used the communication journey not only to become a better speaker, but also for greater self-actualization. And what they had learned had also helped them in their leadership positions in the organization.

As I listened to them that day, I realized that my clearer understanding of their journey was, in fact, pointing me toward the next step on mine—that I should try to give other leaders and aspiring leaders a roadmap for this communication journey.

That's why I wrote this book. I've written two previous books, *Speak Easy* (1978) and *Speak and Get Results* (1983; revised edition, 1994). In the first I gave my readers a greater awareness of the choices they have with their speaking style. I shared my conviction that people can make enormous change in the way they come across to others, once they understand that being an effective speaker doesn't mean changing who they are, but actually becoming more of who they are.

Speak and Get Results drew on my experiences as a business owner and as a communication consultant to business people. It focused on the business demands and business rewards of more effective communication, and included a process for planning content. Working with clients on their style, I had come to realize that they were often unable to organize their material in a way that energized them and got the response they wanted from their listeners.

I wanted to write this book because I wanted to talk about the process of communication development that two decades of working with clients have helped me to understand. I wanted to tell you about the uniqueness of each person's journey, and about the things that all successful journeys have in common. I also wanted to do something even more difficult: to try to articulate the magic that's happened for some people on this journey. The magic that happens not only when you impact the success of your company or make a difference in the lives of others, but also when you feel more fully actualized yourself. I thought it was especially important because, as I've already said, the whole idea of communication training has been turned into a commodity, packaged and simplified until very little of the individual is left. But I believe that real communication development is actually an extraordinarily effective way to become more of who you are, not less. I wanted to give you that message.

So this book is about the communication journey, and those executives who, at some point in their careers, have made a commitment to take that journey. It celebrates the risks they've taken—and the rewards they've received.

I wanted to share with you the insight that they and I have gained in this process. And maybe some of the excitement, too. Because I want you to take your own communication journey, and experience for yourself the power and the joy that come from the connection.

CHAPTER TWO

THE MIRROR AND THE MAGIC WAND

YOU can't really begin a journey without a clear sense of where you're going and how far away it is from where you're starting. You need a destination, a starting point, and some sense of the distance in between.

The communication journey is no different. But, since you're not crossing literal space, it's not so easy to determine your destination, your starting point, and the gap between them. Two images that I've found very useful in helping clients define their journey are the Mirror and the Magic Wand.

Any Mirror will do, as long as it gives you a picture of where you're starting, your current reality. It's an assessment, as objective as possible, of your strengths and weaknesses as a communicator at any given point in time. The Magic Wand is the instrument you use to create a picture of yourself the way you want to be—the destination of your journey.

"MIRROR, MIRROR ON THE WALL"

The Mirror that gives you information about yourself as a communicator can take many forms. Anyone or anything that gives you a "snapshot" of where you are today is a Mirror. And because it's likely to show you some of your weaknesses, you won't always like what you see in the Mirror—like the wicked Queen in "Snow White" who wasn't at all happy to hear that she was no longer the "fairest of them all."

The observations of others can hold up a Mirror to us and become the catalyst for the journey. This is what happened to Dick Measelle, worldwide managing partner of Arthur Andersen. It was 1987, and the firm was at a particularly critical juncture, having just been split into two operating divisions, Andersen Consulting and Arthur Andersen. Dick was chosen to head one of the divisions and he was giving his first speech to the partners as their leader.

"It was a difficult speech," Dick recalls, "for many reasons. I had moved to Chicago and was pretty miserable. I really wasn't even sure I wanted the job. I certainly didn't want the speech, where I was going to be saying things to the partners that I knew they would have a lot of trouble accepting."

Dick went ahead and gave his speech. And got some feedback that turned out to be very significant for him. "One of the leadership partners left a note in my box saying that I wasn't a great speaker but that it was a great speech. In other words, he complimented me on my content but not the delivery. I saw that as only a 50 percent grade, and decided that wasn't nearly good enough." So Dick began to focus on his communication in a way he never had before, and his journey took him, not only into the area of delivery, but also to new approaches even to his content.

The Mirror that this feedback held up to Dick had greater impact on him because of his new leadership position in the firm. As he put it, "You're the leader of a lot of partners and you're up there as their representative. You are them in some real sense of the word. That day your responsibility is to get up in front of those partners as their representative and make them walk away and say, 'I'm glad this guy is the leader right now.' "

The communication journey may begin for you, as it did for Dick, when you move into a new position. You may feel increased pressure on your communication skills to meet your goals, and as a result begin to focus on your weaknesses in this area in a way you hadn't before.

Charlie Frenette got feedback at various times in his career that helped him see his communication more objectively and define areas for development. Charlie remembers one time when a consultant shared some feedback that was especially meaningful —and painful.

He told me that the organization felt we had an over-controlled environment. I had a very hard time dealing with that comment. In fact, I got angry. Not at anybody else, but at myself because it wasn't the way I thought it should be. I had a real hard time processing that—it probably took me a couple of weeks. At first I said that people were just not perceiving this the right way. Eventually I came to the conclusion that I wasn't sending it out the right way.

When I stepped back I saw that I was being inconsistent. On the one hand I was telling everybody that we wanted a safe environment, where it was OK to ask for help and to make a mistake. But then, when people did that, I was cutting them off at the knees. They were feeling ridiculed or reprimanded for not having all the answers. The audio and the video weren't matching at all.

Without that conversation, I'm not sure I would have seen this inconsistency in my communication. My guess is that everyone around me would have continued to nod their heads and say things are fine because they knew that creating a learning environment was important to me. But nothing would have changed.

This account really underlines the painful part of looking in the Mirror. A truly useful Mirror is one that reflects back as honestly or objectively as possible what's there. It doesn't show us what we want to see or tell us what we want to hear. So it takes courage to look into the Mirror, to experience the discomfort, even the pain, that is often the price of self-awareness.

OBSERVING YOURSELF

So how others observe you is one form of the Mirror, sometimes clear and sometimes clouded by hidden agendas. But it's also possible to hold the Mirror up to yourself, and there are various ways of doing that. The Mirror that I've found especially helpful, in both my seminar and consulting work, is the videotape. It's the closest you can get to a picture of what others see and hear when you communicate with them. The video can help bring your subjective impression into a closer alignment with "objective" reality.

Recently I met with the head of a large organization who had expressed an interest in working with me. All I knew was that he was in a leadership position and was giving a lot of talks. When I asked him why he wanted to work with me, he said that he was a pretty good speaker but could probably be better—and that he knew I had worked with a lot of senior people.

Prior to our meeting, I had looked at some videotapes of talks he'd given. My reaction had been that he wasn't "pretty good" and that his listeners probably didn't think so either. In our meeting, he was totally unfocused and didn't really see me. It was clear that this man didn't have an accurate picture of his current reality; so I asked him to watch one of his videotapes with me.

As I was putting the tape in the recorder he acknowledged that he hadn't actually looked at any of the tapes his assistant had sent me: "It felt good when I did it. You know, I'm usually good. I might read too much but basically I'm pretty good."

That executive had simply never looked into the Mirror—until that meeting with me. When he saw the videotape he was clearly uncomfortable. His first reaction was to make excuses, but then he finally just looked at me and said, "Well, it isn't really very good, is it?" And I said, "Let's not talk about good or bad. Let's talk about what it is, specifically, that isn't the way you want it to be." The Mirror had given him a starting place. He had one half of what he needed for his communication journey.

Once again there's that feeling of discomfort looking into the Mirror. But that discomfort can be turned into energy for the journey. That's what happened for Bob Woodson, chairman and CEO of the John H. Harland Company. Bob saw on the videotape a speaker who wasn't focusing on his listeners or showing nearly the degree of commitment to his message that he felt inside—and that a new CEO needed.

> *I didn't realize how bad I was until I saw myself on video when I attended the Speakeasy seminar. It was a rather humiliating experience to see it for the first time, because what I thought was coming across OK turned out not to be once I saw it with my own eyes. Once you see and hear it for yourself, you ei-*

*ther make the commitment to get better or
fade away.*

But the videotape Mirror doesn't only correct a too
rosy inner picture of yourself as a communicator. It
can also correct a too-negative impression of how
you're coming across. Doug Ivester, executive vice
president of Coca-Cola, tends to be tough on himself
and has found the videotape Mirror very useful as a
corrective. "Typically, the tapes that I've looked at
have been better than my mental image was on leav-
ing the room." At that large sales meeting in Hawaii
I saw Doug having a lot more interaction with the
group than I'd seen him have in previous talks. When
I asked him about it later, he acknowledged that the
interaction had been better than he had anticipated,
but also that he really hadn't appreciated how good
it had been until he looked at a videotape of it later.

As Doug shows, using the videotape as a Mirror
is not something you do only at the start of your journey. There are many points along the way where it's
important to get a "reading." To check out where you
are. Videotaping yourself during talks or meetings is
one way of doing this. A few years ago, an executive
who'd just gone through our Senior Executive Seminar sent me a videotape to review. I remember being
impressed that she'd kept her momentum going since
the seminar. But I was even more impressed when I
looked at the tape. She was speaking at an internal
meeting of her people, and she began her remarks this
way:

*Some of you might have noticed the video
camera at the back of the room. Don't worry*

—it's not there for you. It's there for me. I just went through a course in Atlanta and I'm working on some things to improve my communication—which you'll all probably be glad to hear.

I knew right away that this woman was committed to the journey.

So a very valuable form of Mirror is the videotape. But it's not perfect, because, however objective the picture might be that the tape holds up, it's still seen through your eyes. So automatically there's some distortion and interpretation.

Many people, for example, find it difficult to distinguish their inner feelings from their outer impact. One of my clients is a successful businessperson who is very uncomfortable in front of large audiences. At one of our meetings I mentioned a talk he had given some months earlier, where he had actually been quite effective. He said, "But, Sandy, you remember I told you I didn't feel good during that talk."

"Mike, I understand that—but when we looked at the video you agreed that it was better than you had thought, right?" He then said to me, "Well, I never saw the video." But he had! About three months earlier we had sat down together, looked at the video and discussed the changes he'd made. He had totally forgotten our discussion.

Mike is an example of someone whose memory of how he felt when he was giving the talk made it impossible for him to see the picture in the Mirror even months later. That negative feeling created a picture in his head so strong that it literally blocked out the positive picture in the Mirror.

PICTURES IN YOUR HEAD

Our interpretation of what we see in the Mirror is affected by other things besides how we feel. Our values and attitudes affect how we see ourselves. I remember working with a woman who wanted to have more presence and impact when she communicated. When I first saw her, however, she was projecting a very tight, shut-down image to her listeners. At one point during the coaching session I got her to explore loosening up and using herself in a more open and relaxed way. When we looked at her videotape afterward, I saw what to me was a wonderful picture, and I said something like, "Wow! You're being so real and relaxed up there." However, she was looking at herself through different eyes: "But I don't look at all as controlled as the men I work with!"

Her interpretation of the Mirror was influenced by the "oughts" and "shoulds" in her head, accumulated over many years. One of these "shoulds" was that the only way to be professional was to appear like the men around her. This was the picture inside her head that she was trying to match up with the picture in the videotape Mirror. The discrepancy caused her discomfort, but in her case that discomfort turned out to be constructive. It stimulated her to examine the picture in her head and determine if it was an obstacle on her journey—if, in other words, her sense of how she should look and sound was blocking her progress toward her goal.

There's a very complex and creative relationship between the picture in the Mirror and the pictures inside your head of how you think you're communicating or how you think you ought to communicate.

Sometimes the picture in the Mirror creates an incongruity with one in your head. Any good Mirror will often do this, whether it's videotape, feedback, questions, or even observation of your own behavior. This lack of congruence produces discomfort, and the discomfort can lead to self-examination. That's what happened for Charlie as a result of his consultant's feedback. His initial reaction of anger came from the incongruity between how he thought he was communicating and the picture he was given of how his communication was experienced by his team.

Sometimes the picture in the Mirror, when it shows you things you don't like or that you want to change, actually matches a picture in your head. In other words, you see in the Mirror the effect of some of your assumptions and beliefs about communication. Here the congruence itself leads to an examination of the inner picture, to better understand what's inside you that's helping to create that picture out there you don't like. That's what happened for Amy White, a vice president of Coca-Cola USA. She saw herself on the videotape in the seminar as a woman who was not as confident as she wanted to be, and who was being careful and controlled in the way she was relating to her listeners. She didn't like this picture, but it stimulated her to examine her inner picture of the communication situation. What she discovered was that the Mirror was a logical consequence of some of her assumptions:

> *I took a big step forward in confidence and ability because I suddenly realized some of the things that had been getting in the way. I had*

been seeing the whole communication situa-
tion wrong. I had been seeing it as a threat:
that I was out there in public being judged by
all these people, and as a result I had built
almost a wall between myself and my listen-
ers. Once I was able to shift the paradigm and
see myself as sharing something that would
be helpful to these people I began to get rid of
that wall. It was wonderful.

"Wonderful." This is the authentic experience of someone getting closer to those ultimate goals of connecting more with herself and with others. Amy's wall had confined her and separated her from her listeners. Removing it was part of her personal growth, but it also produced some very tangible business results for her.

As you continue your journey, you'll become more and more used to, even eager for, the pictures of your current reality that a Mirror can provide. You'll use them to develop awareness of what works for you as a communicator. They become the new pictures in your head, more accurate and more energizing. With their help, you'll begin to identify certain feelings and physical cues within yourself, or signs from your listeners, that tell you you're on course toward one of your communication goals. And at this point you'll begin to use another Mirror: the communication situation itself, while it's actually in progress. Right in the middle of a presentation or a conversation, you'll be able to pull back and notice whether those feelings or cues or signs are present. You become, momentarily, an observer of yourself and the other as if each were a Mirror, and you assess the quality or effectiveness of the communication. Then you make adjustments as necessary.

Amy White feels that one of her greatest helps in moving her toward her communication goals is her ability "to check in with myself to see how I'm doing. It may be making a conscious decision to check on my breathing or just check on how connected I feel with the people I'm talking to."

Coke CFO Jack Stahl used this on-the-spot Mirror to make adjustments in the middle of a development discussion with someone in his division. He had begun the discussion with an offhand remark about the other person's being a bit cynical. Over the next couple of minutes it became clear to Jack that his remark was having a very negative impact on the conversation:

> *I was going nowhere. He would give me very top-line answers to my questions. He was sitting way back in his chair. At that point I made the decision to stop and share with him what I was feeling. "Gee, this conversation seems real uncomfortable for you and me." He picked right up on it: "You're right. Your comment made me feel like it wasn't a risk-free environment." I assured him I hadn't meant to do that. So we sort of disengaged and started over.*

Jack's story illustrates two important things. One is the value of using the Mirror, which here was that moment of stepping back and evaluating the situation. The other is the risk Jack took in sharing what he saw. Sometimes you have to take a risk to establish a connection. Jack did exactly that, and it paid off.

THE MIRROR ISN'T A "JUDGE"

In order to use the Mirror effectively, as a starting place or checkpoint for your journey, it's not enough simply to get a picture (to hear the feedback, to see the videotape, to observe yourself). The data it provides must become information before you can use it. First of all, it's very important that you, or anyone helping you on your journey, avoid interpreting the Mirror in judgmental terms. One of the things I have always tried not to do with clients is to ask them, "Is it good or bad?" It's amazing how many people want to react in these terms, as if there were some ideal model or absolute standard for communication. But "good" or "bad" doesn't give you anything specific to change, and the very terms can sap the confidence you'll need in order to change.

Instead, the Speakeasy process gives people some very broad criteria to evaluate themselves as communicators in a non-judgmental way. In the area of style, these are the qualities of authority, energy, awareness of your audience, and reaching out. For content, we use, among others, the concepts of "Point X," "hidden X's," "assumptions," and "message."* These qualities and concepts have evolved out of my

---

* These concepts are described at length in my second book, *Speak and Get Results.*

work with many people, as I saw some of the broad and recurring areas that people needed to work on. Their purpose is not to serve as "rules," but to give people a vocabulary or a framework to help them objectify and then evaluate in a useful way what they see in the Mirror, beyond "good" or "bad" or "like" and "don't like." If any particular quality or concept is undeveloped or even not present at all, you immediately have potential areas to work on.

USING FEEDBACK AS A MIRROR

Feedback from other people can really help you make progress on your journey. When you're using feedback as your Mirror, it's important that this picture, too, be presented to you in a useful form. Sometimes, in the case of unsolicited feedback, you can't control this. But if you ask for feedback be as specific as you can about what you want. For example, don't ask, "How did I do?" or "Was it okay?" Instead, ask for information that can help you with your goal, such as:

- Did I answer those questions in a direct, concise way?
- I was trying to get across one very important message. Did I succeed?
- Did I seem to be really open to the suggestions that were being made?
- I'm working on taking more time when I talk— slowing down, pausing, really looking in control. Did it come across that way to you?

Feedback is only really useful when it's asked for—and given—in relation to a specific goal. The responses you get to specific requests like the ones above are much more likely to help you on your journey, and they'll also make it easier for the other person to hold up the Mirror. Many people, especially if they're in subordinate positions, aren't comfortable giving negative feedback. So the picture in their Mirror is distorted by their concern to be kind or to be safe. They're more likely to give you their honest assessment if you focus them on a specific aspect of your communication and let them react to a behavior rather than to whether or not you "were okay."

As useful as feedback from others can be, I've found it can be limited as a Mirror, especially for those in leadership positions. Feedback becomes less objective, less honest. In the last few years, as I've coached presidents of companies or heads of divisions —people with teams around them—it has become very clear that the feedback they get is rarely "clean." The individuals on the team bring their own agendas, which are heavily influenced by their own history of dealing with people they were subordinate to or people who were authority figures for them. Their feedback comes out of their personal and political needs and their wishes about how the leader should be to make them comfortable. It's not necessarily what's best for the leader or for the company. Or even relevant to who the leader actually is.

It isn't that these needs shouldn't be considered. It's just that feedback that comes out of those needs will often present you with a distorting Mirror. It will offer a picture of what someone else wants you to be.

You should be wary of others who want to define your journey for you rather than help you define it for yourself.

The higher you go in an organization the more difficult it is to get good feedback. As Roy Bostock, the chairman of the international advertising firm D'Arcy Masius Benton & Bowles, observes, "In my experience as CEO, you don't get a lot of instantaneous, automatic feedback. I don't get that unless I ask for it. When I do, I have to make sure I ask people who are not going to blow smoke."

Doug Ivester agrees:

> *I think the higher up you go in an organization, the more the feedback is muted and cautious. Leaders must develop mechanisms of feedback that allow them to get the facts on their own performance and communication styles. It's a very complex thing. If you don't realize how complex it is, you run the risk of significantly under- or over-evaluating your own performance. You have to learn to read signals of feedback as opposed to just accepting direct feedback.*

In my experience, one of the things that make feedback so difficult for executives to deal with is that it's often related to their strength; usually they're being told, in various ways, that they're going too far with their strength. Their natural, initial reaction to this is something like, "Well, damn, these people don't want me to come on so strong, but they do want me to drive the company ahead, don't they?" So at first they don't want to listen, mainly because they don't know what to do with the feedback. They're afraid that if they listen to it they'll have to change who they are and what's made them successful.

At this point it's most important to get back in touch with yourself and with someone who can help you sort all this out. In fact, Frank Cella, the president of Nestlé Canada, came to my Senior Executive Seminar to do exactly that. He had reached the presidency of his company and felt a need to "get in touch with my own essence, if you will. I really felt I needed something like that because I was getting so many conflicting comments and so much confusing feedback from other people that if I tried to satisfy every piece of it I'd end up a pretzel."

Frank illustrates the special problem that feedback can pose for senior executives who have just entered a new stage in their careers or taken on new responsibilities. They've been on a plateau for a while and gotten comfortable. Then all of a sudden there are new demands, including communication demands, and what they were doing before doesn't seem good enough. They're a little shaky, trying to decide on their next goal, and there are a lot of people around them who have ideas about what and how they should be. It's at this point that they're likely to be especially vulnerable to and confused by feedback, and in need of a safe place to sound off and get back in touch with themselves. This is essential, because I believe you can't really deal with and effectively use the feedback of others unless you're connected with yourself—and unless you trust that connection.

However complex getting reliable feedback may

be, if you process it in this context of trust it can be a useful Mirror for you. And I include trust not only in yourself, but also in the person giving you the feedback. Both are essential.

Your communication journey is no different from your life journey or your business career. As you progress and grow you develop greater awareness of who you are—your strengths,' weaknesses, your growth areas. When you've seen enough Mirror pictures on your communication journey, you gain trust in yourself and your ability to evaluate the Mirror that others hold up to you. You develop your own process for dealing with their feedback. Here's the way Harry Caulfield, the executive director of The Permanente Medical Group, describes his:

> Sometimes the feedback hurts, but that's okay. You know there are a lot of judgments involved, both from the one making the critique and from yourself receiving it. So the first thing I do is acknowledge that it hurts. Then I drop it for a day. I come back later and analyze what was said: What specifically was being criticized? Was it a behavior, a style, part of the message?
>
> Then I consider if the comment is valid, and one criterion I use is whether I've heard it before, if it hits a counter inside me. If I decide it's valid, then I deal with it. But I might not deal with it immediately, because I also decide how important it is in relation to all the other things I'm trying to accomplish.

*You just can't deal with everything at the
same time.*

Larry Weinbach, the CEO at Arthur Andersen, uses
his trust in himself to evaluate feedback from others:

*Within a partnership you get much more feed-
back than you would in a corporate environment. If you're going to be successful you
can't let your ego get in the way of your common sense. I know my strengths and weaknesses better than anyone, and I believe I'm
honest with myself.*

*So when you get feedback, you weigh it
against your own perception. If you sit back
and say you have no weaknesses you're kid-
ding yourself, and if you don't understand
your strengths and play off them, you're kid-
ding yourself, too. I use my own self-evalua-
tion as the guidepost on which I test the
feedback.*

I think that George Shaheen, the worldwide managing partner of Andersen Consulting, nicely summarizes much of what I've been saying about a leader's
problems with feedback: the different agendas of
those giving it, the confusion of the person receiving
it. And George, too, depends on his self-awareness to
sort through it all:

*A lot of people give feedback to a person in
my position for different reasons, and you can*

become very confused. What one person sees as a strength someone else sees as a weakness. What one person sees as a message someone else sees as a signal. With all this different feedback it's easy to become defensive.

Most people in leadership positions are there because they want to make the organization better, they care about the people, they want to leave a legacy of progress, they want to be well-regarded and respected. So when people start critiquing you with a microscope, it's tough on your view of yourself. It can affect your courage. But you can get by that as long as you know in your heart you're doing what you think is right.

So successful executives and effective leaders are open to feedback; they use it to explore where they are both intellectually and emotionally, and how that relates to who they want to be and need to be in their world; but they don't let it shape who they are. They know that all the really important answers are inside themselves.

But trust in the source of feedback is also an important element, if you're going to be able to use feedback as a reliable Mirror. It's got to come from someone you believe isn't "blowing smoke." That trust is usually built over time, with a specific colleague, a friend, a coach. But time alone isn't enough; the trust comes from a deep sense that the other person really sees you and wants for you what you want for yourself.

I've used many coaches in my life, many people

who gave me feedback. They have been people I felt saw me, understood who I was at that moment in time, and accepted it (not thought it was perfect, but accepted it). They were people who were able to hear and see where I was struggling to go and who, I thought, brought some expertise to help me get there. But if they only brought the expertise and didn't make me feel that they truly saw me as an individual, then I didn't accept their feedback and pretty soon stopped using them.

There aren't many people who see us like that, and it's tough to find them inside your own organization. That's why an outsider, a consultant or coach, can often be a more useful Mirror in your communication journey. Remember that it was an outsider who gave Charlie Frenette that significant feedback on the "overcontrolled environment" he was creating. I try to bring the same level of awareness to my clients that I expect other coaches or consultants to bring to me. I believe that they accept some pretty direct, even tough, feedback from me because they sense that I truly see who they are and who they want to be. As least that's what Frank Cella felt when he worked with me in the Senior Executive Seminar:

> I understood from the first day that you weren't trying to change my style, my energy level or my presentation technique. You were trying to let the real me come out. I think you saw something in me that you were trying to help me bring out. So I knew that you saw the whole me, not just the tough me, the tense me, the focused me, but the whole me.

We will trust the Mirror when, and only when, we believe it really sees us.

So the Mirror is an essential item for your communication journey. It gives you a picture, an honest assessment of where you're starting and of your progress along the way. Looking into the Mirror is part of your personal growth as well, because it is often uncomfortable. The person truly committed to the journey uses the Mirror frequently, getting better and better at seeing what's there and asking for what he or she needs to know. And in dealing with it.

The Mirror may show you where you are now and suggest a direction for improvement. But by itself it's not enough to get you started on your journey. You need the other essential item.

THE MAGIC WAND

It's important to be as objective as possible about yourself when you're looking in the Mirror. But forget objectivity when you've got the Magic Wand in your hand. It's the instrument of your desire. Use it to create a picture of yourself as the communicator you want to be.

Let me emphasize the word *you*. The picture you create with the Magic Wand is not what you think you ought to be or what others have said you should be. That picture has to come out of you, because it's the goal of your journey and you won't have the energy to work toward it unless it is truly what you want, your heart's desire. Doug Ivester puts it exactly right:

I really think that to be an effective communicator you've got to have your own expectations. Because if you're trying to live up to the expectations of others, you're not really in control of the vision. When you have a vision for yourself, you're better able to enhance your skills to achieve it.

I've learned a lot myself over the years about the importance of having the goal come out of each person. I believe that I've always been good at looking at a person and seeing the possibilities. I can often get an immediate picture of where they could be as communicators five years down the road. Years ago, when I started my business, I'd take this picture and start pushing them toward it as hard as I could.

I got different responses from that. Some people were relieved and quite comfortable to put themselves in the hands of an "expert" who would tell them where to go and how to get there. But there were others who didn't want to be pushed and resisted me. They felt I wasn't really seeing them.

Today I try to do it differently. I won't let people make me the expert or the enemy. If I set the goal of the journey I am limiting the potential of what can come out of them and the degree of commitment they'll have to reach that goal.

Still, getting people to see the possibilities and to say what they want in any aspect of their lives isn't easy, and the same is true for their communication. Many people get very bogged down in the present. For example, they'll say, "Well, you know, I've never had any experience at this." Or, "I'm a fifty-year-old engineer and I can't do this." Or, "I'm just not outgoing." Or, "English is my second language." All of their comments have to do with where they are now. I've found the image of the Magic Wand very effective in helping people to let go of their current reality. "If you could have it any way you want, what would it be? What is your fantasy? Wave the Magic Wand. What result do you want?"

When George Shaheen became the leader of a newly created, 18,000-person organization in 1989, he was too busy building the infrastructure that would drive the firm forward to worry about communication. He began to work on his speaking only because of the pressure of a large meeting. George admits that when he began that work he didn't have a Magic Wand picture: "You can't go toward something when you don't know what it is." In the beginning, George allowed me to push him. I challenged him to create an ambitious Magic Wand picture. He describes that early relationship this way:

> I didn't know where I was going with my speaking. So it was more like somebody yanking you out of bed, making you get dressed and go to the office. Left to yourself, you just might sleep in.

George didn't need to be pushed for long. When he saw progress on his videotapes, he quickly appreciated the possibilities and made a commitment far beyond what he initially thought would be needed.

Often the first try at a Magic Wand picture needs revision or adjustment. Just as the picture in the Mirror has to give you useful information, your goal needs to be defined in a way that allows you to identify the components necessary to make it a reality. Otherwise its value will be limited. I often do a lot of probing and questioning around that initial picture until the client describes it in a way that will give focus and direction to her journey. For example, Harry Caulfield was very clear about what was his goal and what wasn't.

> *What I was not interested in was whether my right hand should go up at five seconds and my left down at thirty seconds. I had had experience with that type of approach and it turned me off. I wanted to be able to communicate effectively for the purpose of improving the organization.*

This picture needed filling out. What did Harry mean by "communicate effectively"? In what ways did he want to "improve the organization" and what would his communication have to look like to do that? It was only after that kind of probing and questioning that Harry had a Magic Wand picture that he could use to set out on his journey.

Roy Bostock expressed his Magic Wand picture in terms of what his organization needed: "Communications that can bring a global enterprise together, with shared values, principles, practices, and points of view." This picture, great as it is, also raises some questions that need to be answered before it is individualized enough to be really useful for Roy's personal journey; questions like "What are those values and principles?" "What would your own communication look like if it were exemplifying those values?"

Occasionally the problem with the Magic Wand picture isn't that it needs to be more specific or individualized. The problem is the picture itself. This usually happens for one of two reasons: either the Magic Wand picture is too far away from the picture in the Mirror, the current reality, or it is too close, sometimes identical with it. In each case the journey is compromised. When the goal is too far away, there's the danger of frustration and giving up. When the goal is virtually a version of where you already are, there's no room for a journey.

Dealing with this problem can be a very delicate matter, because, as I've said, I now make every effort to go with the client's goal and not with my goal for him. However, one of the things I have an obligation to be is honest. So if I have strong reservations about the Magic Wand picture, I'll usually say so. I'm more likely to do that when it's too close to the Mirror picture. In the case of the too-far-away picture, I try to get the client to define some intermediate goals that I know will allow him or her success and satisfaction. As long as you're making progress toward that Magic Wand picture, it doesn't matter if your reach exceeds your grasp.

But it's different when the client doesn't see the gap. This happens when he has no real awareness of his current reality, of how he's coming across to others. He hasn't taken an honest look in the Mirror. So, for example, if someone has a reputation for being cold, tough, and arrogant, and his Magic Wand picture is to be even more authoritative, I will try to find a way to let that person see he is already conveying an image that has gone too far in that direction. Mainly I will try to hold the Mirror up to his Magic Wand picture, through feedback of my impressions or video-taping or probing questions.

So you've got a goal for your journey, one you can believe in and work with, and you've got a picture of where you're starting from. The next step is to compare your two pictures: the one of your current reality that you see in the Mirror, and the picture of your desire created by the Magic Wand. That comparison helps you identify specific skills or issues to be worked on to close the gap between the two pictures. That work is your journey.

The skills that will help you close that gap may include basic techniques like breathing or articulation, interpersonal skills like listening, thinking skills like focusing and organizing. The issues may include things like personal power, openness, awareness of others, taking risk, developing a point of view. These become the stages of your journey, the opportunities and the challenges you'll face on the way toward the picture your Magic Wand has created.

When Bob Woodson compared his two pictures, this is what he saw: "It was the difference between being the 'aw, shucks' good ol' boy and being the leader who communicates his message with commitment." To close this gap, he identified some areas he needed to work on, such as bringing more energy to his delivery, and developing a more message-focused content.

TODAY'S MAGIC WAND, TOMORROW'S MIRROR

In the first chapter I expressed my belief that the ultimate goal of the communication journey is greater and deeper connection with yourself and others. This is an ultimate goal, never fully reached or sustained for any of us. We may have moments of profound connection with others and moments when we feel fully actualized in our communication. These moments confirm our belief and strengthen our desire for that ultimate goal of connection. But they pass.

The picture that the Magic Wand creates is meant to be a stretch, but not unattainable. We're directed toward it by some pretty specific personal or business need. The journey never ends, not because the goal isn't reached, but because the goal changes. One way of describing the shape or progress of the journey is that the picture you create with the Magic Wand today is the picture you want to see in the Mirror tomorrow. Once the goal is achieved, it becomes the current reality for your communication, the place you set out from as you move toward your next goal.

I've worked with clients over enough years to witness and be a part of this progress. I've seen the goals achieved and the goals changed. I've seen the Magic Wand become the Mirror.

I remember Amy White. When she came to the Speakeasy seminar in 1982, her Magic Wand picture focused only on her comfort:

> *I wanted speaking in front of a group not to be so painful for me. I didn't have a picture yet that "this could be terrific. This is some-*

thing I could get really excited about and have a lot of impact with." All I wanted was more understanding of what I'd call the technique so that I could feel more in control in that situation.

Amy worked on "the technique" and reached her goal of being more in control when she spoke. She created new Magic Wand pictures, and today she's focusing more on interpersonal relationships and individual, one-on-one communication. Here's how she describes her current goal: "My goal is honest and open communication. And I understand now that to achieve that I've got be willing to talk about things that aren't easy for me, especially my own feelings." The comparison between those two goals, ten years apart, gives you some sense of how far Amy's journey has taken her.

Doug Ivester has traveled some distance, too. As the young CFO of a very large corporation, Doug was trying to define himself in the job. When he waved his Magic Wand then, in the early eighties, he created this picture: "I wanted to accept that being myself was good enough, and I wanted a communication style that was me, not somebody else." A later goal focused more on his content: he wanted to develop financial presentations that were not just a recital of facts and numbers, but expressed a definite point of view.

Like Amy, when Jim Fischer, the head of the Technology Services Group at Andersen Consulting, began his journey he was concerned with his comfort. He wanted to feel good when he was speaking to his people, and he knew that increasing his awareness of himself and of his listeners was a crucial part of this goal. Later, after that Magic Wand picture had become the Mirror, he set himself a new goal:

> *Every time I face a communication task now, I want to use it as an opportunity for movement and improvement—an opportunity for me to assist my listeners to move to where it's better for them and the firm to be.*

So with the help of these two tools or images, the Mirror and the Magic Wand, you can define your communication journey and measure your progress on it. It takes courage to look into the first and faith in yourself—your ability to grow and change—to use the second. Those who are successful in their journey have a gallery of Magic Wand pictures that have turned into Mirrors, dreams that came true. Those pictures are the record of their journey.

Each person creates his or her own individual goals. And the journey, although it takes place in the world of business needs and business results, is very much a personal journey. But after many years of helping people on it, I've noticed that successful journeys tend to set similar goals in roughly the same order. In other words, there seems to be an underlying pattern common to successful communication development. We could call that pattern the Journey with a capital "J." It needs a chapter all its own.

CHAPTER THREE

THE JOURNEY

PEOPLE who begin work on their speaking don't see themselves as starting on a long-term journey. They usually begin because of the demands of a particular situation or a new role. Perhaps they've advanced to a senior position and have to present to the board for the first time. Or they have become the president of a national association and have to address the annual convention. Or they're introducing a new product to distributors.

As they work on their speaking for that new situation or that new role, they get a sense of what is possible for them, both personally and professionally. They begin to want more. So, little by little, their whole attitude toward communication changes: what they had looked at only as a skill becomes a passion; what had been only a tool for accomplishing their job becomes the core of the job itself.

Whatever the particular stimulus that initiates the journey, it's usually something that makes you aware of your own discomfort. Because of that discomfort you feel that you're not responding as successfully or functioning as effectively as you would like. So the journey typically begins with an unwelcome focus on the self and a felt need to build up confidence for a challenge ahead.

MAGIC WAND PICTURE #1: COMFORTABLE, EFFECTIVE

John Hunter came to the Atlanta headquarters of Coca-Cola from the presidency of Coca-Cola Japan, one of the company's most important markets. His journey began when he realized, to his surprise, that he wasn't as comfortable communicating, especially to large groups, as he had been before:

> *The biggest surprise was that I didn't handle it, at least initially, as well as I thought I was going to. I felt that I had handled this kind of communication better when I was in operating roles. Maybe it was more stressful in the Atlanta environment. In any case, it just*

didn't come to me as easily as I had hoped it would.

So the Magic Wand picture that John first set for himself was to feel comfortable and in control when he got up to talk.

John's experience is fairly common for very successful executives who move into new leadership positions. Suddenly they feel a discomfort that either they had never felt before or that they had long ago found some way to control. This is what happened to Roy Bostock when he assumed greater responsibilities in his world-wide organization:

> *I had done a lot of speaking but had really never thought about what I was doing. I just kind of stood up and started talking; and, as most of us do when we're young, aggressive and successful, we think everybody's listening to everything we say and it's all wonderful.*

> *Then one day I woke up and found myself very nervous standing in front of people. I knew that had to be dealt with because, quite aside from the personal discomfort, you just can't communicate when you're thinking more about yourself than your listeners.*

So the first Magic Wand picture will usually express wishes such as, "I want to feel more comfortable"; "I want to look more relaxed"; "I want to have the confidence in front of people that I used to have." These are often the wishes of executives with solid records of accomplishment and significant expertise in their business or industry; yet a change in their circumstances produces a crisis in confidence. They begin to feel that the best of who and what they are just isn't coming across when they communicate.

Tim Haas had first worked on his speaking skills when he was the vice-president of sales at Coca-Cola Foods. At that point he had a lot of confidence as a communicator based on years of successful experience motivating and training people to carry on a sales mission. All he wanted initially from Speakeasy was some techniques that would give him sufficient confidence that he would not need to memorize his stand-up presentations. But Tim's journey actually began a few years later, when "I woke up one morning and all of a sudden I was CEO."

> *To say that I was overwhelmed when this opportunity came along is really an understatement, because I wasn't expecting it, didn't plan on it, couldn't even see it coming. So I went through a period when I believed that somebody had made a significant mistake and, in point of fact, was really wondering if I should go back and say, "Look, I think you guys made a mistake and I'm not capable of doing this."*

Communication became a core issue then for Tim, as he struggled to become comfortable with his new role and to express himself with the confidence of a leader. It was at this point that he began to see that the techniques he had learned a few years earlier in the Senior Executive Seminar were only the first step on his communication journey.

At this first stage of the journey, the Mirror usually confirms that your Magic Wand goal of comfort and confidence is right on target. You look at a videotape, for example, and see a person who's using her body in a tight way or a careful way, or in a casual way that's an attempt to disguise discomfort. You hear a voice that mumbles or races, that doesn't seem to own the words. The Mirror shows you none of the commitment you feel inside, little of the presence that your title suggests and your responsibilities require.

That's what people usually see in the Mirror when they look at their style or delivery, at *how* they communicate their message. And their initial work focuses on changing that picture, especially through the use of some basic physical and vocal skills. They explore ways to occupy and move through their physical space with more ease and authority. They learn ways to use their energy, which is often locked up in the form of physical tension, to help them express the commitment they feel inside. They learn how to use their own breathing to control their nervousness and to support a fuller voice. And they explore the power in the pause.

The use of these basic style techniques doesn't depend on the cooperation or response of a listener. They are things you as the speaker can do for yourself. And once you've mastered them they are yours forever—a consistent and reliable source of confidence for any communication situation, from an audience of thousands to a tough, one-on-one negotiation. Now the Mirror shows you an image that looks and sounds more like the person you feel inside. Your confidence soars.

Jack Stahl describes the effect of learning these skills: "Fear of not having the appropriate communication skills can create an awful energy, a negative energy that keeps you in a very narrowly defined corridor. You knock down that fear through building some skills, you practice the skills until they become comfortable. Then you can move on to the next level."

But this focus on self, on being more confident and in control, isn't confined only to style or delivery skills. Most people find that an important part of feeling confident and in control in a communication situation is the result of being in control of their content, of *what* they say. This works two ways. If they are clear about what they want to accomplish and have selected their content with a view toward accomplishing it, they come into the situation with more confidence and security. Their listeners are then more likely to perceive them as having the authority of ownership and the energy of a direction.

So, along with those basic style techniques, the mental discipline of setting a clear, single objective is a key step on the way to reaching that first Magic Wand picture of a confident, in-control communicator. In the Speakeasy planning process we call this discipline "defining your Point X." The worldwide managing partners of both business units of Arthur Andersen & Co, SC testify to the difference that this kind of content focus makes for them. Here's George Shaheen of Andersen Consulting:

> *You are more apt to be successful in your communication if you figure out where you*

*want your audience to be when you're done
and then select the content that will help get
them there. Unless you do that, you can have
all the style techniques working for you, but
you still won't reach as high a level as you
want or feel as comfortable doing it.*

Notice that George associates comfort with this planning skill—we're still in the area of focusing on yourself. His counterpart Dick Measelle, of Arthur Andersen, echoes George's emphasis on the importance of having a clear focus for your content:

*I've worked hard not to clutter up my talks
with a bunch of different messages, but rather
to have one central theme I can hammer away
at. People can take something away, as opposed to my speech being a cafeteria line
where there are a hundred things to select
from and nobody really knows what the overall message is. I used to feel that my talks
were sort of like travelogues—interesting and
truthful maybe, but missing the mark because
there was no focus.*

*Now the days when I speak are good days.
I really look forward to getting up there and
pouring myself into something I really want
to get across. I still get nervous, but it's more
adrenaline than tension now.*

Energy and confidence come when you're clear on what you want to accomplish with your content.

I think the example of Bob Woodson nicely summarizes the elements of this first stage of the journey: the pressures that a new position puts on both the content and the style of your communication. Bob was fifty-eight when he was appointed president of the John H. Harland Company and the designated successor to the CEO. He had been with the company for twenty years and had risen through the ranks on the financial side of the business. He knew that his communication responsibilities would be significantly greater, and different.

> *I had been basically in the shadow of my predecessor. While we had made joint presentations my part had always been of a financial nature, quoting and indicating figures rather than trying to convey a message.*

> *But now I was facing two new challenges with my communication: who I'd be talking to and what I'd be talking about. I'd be making more presentations to the outside world— shareholders, analysts—where I was the company spokesman. And internally, I'd be speaking to all the employee groups. And when I spoke I would be representing the company with them, too. With both of these audiences my effectiveness would depend on my personal credibility.*

> *And then the content of what I was saying would be different. Rather than talking numbers and financial results, I would be speaking in terms of the company's mission: the vision*

we have, what we want the company to be,
what our strategic plans are, and why we're
making the moves we're making today. You're
really talking about the future.

Bob understood what a significant shift this was for him, and how essential his communication was going to be in his new leadership role at Harland. So he stepped out of the shadow of his predecessor and began his communication journey, because he wanted to project the confidence and command that his new position required.

In my experience this is the usual first stage of the communication journey: an intense focus on the self in an effort to reach a goal of greater comfort and confidence. This first stage might occur at any point in a person's career—a young account executive in her first job, the newly elected president of a local club, or, as we've seen, a high-level executive with years of success behind him. Whenever you begin, you reach that goal of comfort and confidence by developing greater self-awareness in the areas of style and content—exploring style techniques that make you feel more in control and that project authority and energy to your listeners and learning the content discipline of defining what specifically you want to accomplish in each communication situation.

By the end of this stage of the journey you know that you have choices in the way you come across to others, and you know that exercising those choices is in your control. The Mirror begins to confirm that others are seeing the same in-charge, committed communicator that you feel yourself to be inside. Now you're ready to create a new Magic Wand picture and shift the focus from yourself. You're ready to deal with the listener.

MAGIC WAND PICTURE #2: PERSUASIVE

Making something happen, getting a result—this is what a business leader wants from his communication, and he deals with his discomfort first because he experiences it as an obstacle to his effectiveness. But because he knows that accomplishing his objective depends on others—their input, support, understanding—he very soon shifts his focus to his listeners. Jack Stahl is clear on both the timing and the motivation for this shift:

> *Once you begin to feel comfortable with the basic tools, and you see that people perceive you as being in control, then you begin to appreciate what a little input can do for you. By input I mean understanding what's happening with the people you're communicating with. You realize how much more effective you can be with the input.*

To reach this new Magic Wand picture of being effective or persuasive, you begin to develop awareness of your listeners. In the area of style or delivery, this means, first of all, the simple act of seeing them. After all, you can't get input from them if you don't see them. This is usually described as the technique of eye contact, but I try to avoid that phrase because too often it's a mechanical activity performed by a speaker to create the illusion that she's seeing her listeners. The actual attention is still on self. Really seeing your listeners, on the other hand, means being out there with them, looking for responses and reactions to what you're saying. Do they get it? Are you on track with them? Are they okay with this?

This can be a little scary in the early stages of the journey. You may see things that you don't want to see, such as disagreement, puzzlement, or even boredom. But unless you see these reactions you can't make the adjustments necessary to reach your objective for the communication situation. So you take one of the many risks that are an inevitable part of the journey. You look. You see.

The shift begins simply, by making an effort to maintain visual focus on a single listener until you've expressed one idea or thought. Though the initial practice of this may feel mechanical, the purpose is to be sure that you've actually stayed long enough with each person to give them something they can react to or acknowledge if they wish.

As you become more aware of the other, something very interesting happens. You'll probably increase your comfort and confidence. This is an important feature of the journey: although the stages are progressive, they're not absolutely linear in the sense that you never revisit a previous stage. The experience of later stages deepens understanding of earlier issues, reinforces the value of some techniques, and at times gives you a new perspective on something you thought you understood. Seeing your listeners, here in the second stage, is a good example. Most people need some degree of confidence and comfort to risk it, but once they do, what they see often increases their comfort and confidence. This happens for two reasons: first, the simple fact of doing it, of choosing to take the risk, is an expression of the speaker's being in control, exercising a choice. Second, once you actually see your listeners, they usually don't turn out to be the hostile, critical people you imagined. And this experience boosts your confidence. Amy White recalls what happened to her when she took the risk of focusing on her listeners:

> *The first two sentences were really hard, being up there in front of all those people. I can feel that way right now when I remember it. But as soon as I saw people in the group and saw the reaction I was getting, it was great. I really felt like I was talking to people. Even now I can describe the looks on people's faces as I was talking.*
>
> *You actually start redefining your listeners. They're not all sitting there as judges and critics. They're people you're having a conversation with about things that really matter to you.*

Just as in the first stage, there is a content component of this stage as well. In the initial stage you asked yourself what you wanted out of a communication situation. This self-questioning, to arrive at a clear focus, is not always easy. You've got to figure out and then state out loud what it is you really want. But unless your partners in the communication also want it, you're not likely to get it. So in this next stage you analyze your listeners in terms of the objective you want to accomplish and begin a process of putting yourself in their shoes. This process opens up the eventual possibility of connection far beyond this second stage of the journey. At this point, however, consideration of your listeners is mainly within the context of your own objective. You want to know what values or interests they have that would motivate them to reach it. The product of this analysis, in our Speakeasy planning process, is the Message—a statement of the listeners' stake in the speaker's objective, expressed in the listeners' language and from their perspective.*

And just as seeing the other in your delivery tends to reinforce the confidence you developed from the initial focus on yourself, this examination of the needs and perspective of the other actually increases your own self-awareness. You uncover your own attitudes and assumptions about your listeners which, although not always accurate and rarely examined, have shaped your communication in the past. You begin to develop a healthy skepticism about what you think you know about others.

Now you have greater awareness of the other, as a result of going further with both style and content skills. You're starting to experience greater effectiveness in your communication, and greater consistency in the results you're getting. Many people could, and

* There is a complete discussion of these concepts in the first section of *Speak and Get Results*.

do, stop here. But not everybody. Some, now that they've begun to experience the possibilities, both of self- and other-awareness, want more. They're ready to create another Magic Wand picture.

MAGIC WAND PICTURE #3: TRUSTED AND TRUSTING

From this point on in the journey you're advancing on two fronts: continuing to explore and express yourself, and reaching out more to others. You focus more on your communication with small groups and individuals because you know that your success, whatever your function or business, depends on relationships—with clients and customers, with members of your team. And relationships are built on trust. Your new Magic Wand picture, then, will concentrate on those aspects of communication that build trust: honesty and directness in your own communication, and listening better to others.

One of the major ways to increase the honesty and directness in your communication is by giving more attention to the idea of "point of view." People want to get a sense of where others are coming from when they interact on any particular issue. So it's important to develop a point of view and be willing to state it, not in an insensitive, authoritarian, or inflexible way, but in a way that leaves people clear about your position and your process. Each of these is important, as Larry Weinbach makes clear: "As a leader I have to be sure to express my point of view. And, particularly in a partnership, where partners tend to be more outspoken than the corporate firm, it's important for people to appreciate your thought process as well. You want to develop and maintain a reputation for being thoughtful." Articulating a position gives others a point of reference, something to relate to even if they disagree. Letting them in on the process helps them perceive your consistency in approaching issues. Without consistency there is no trust.

Larry's colleagues echo him on both these aspects. George Shaheen clearly sees articulating a point of view as one of his main responsibilities: "I've always had strong convictions about who I was, what I was, and what I believed in. I was never hesitant to share those. Even when they don't like what you say, people want to know what you think, feel, and experience. Honesty is very important."

Dick Measelle, George's counterpart at Arthur Andersen, emphasizes the importance of letting people in on the process by which you arrive at your point of view, so that they can perceive your consistency.

> It's disturbing to work with other leaders within the firm or with senior people from other organizations when you don't know where they're coming from or where they're likely to come from. Not that you can predict all actions or positions, but you ought to be able to form an impression of someone that includes an ability to predict how they're going to react in certain circumstances. And when they don't do that, when they bounce all

over the place, that raises a real question about what's going on with them—and how much you can depend on them.

It's especially important for leaders to be able to develop and express a clear point of view. Others expect it of them. Larry Weinbach feels that "if you know of corporations where people were able to move ahead without a point of view, you ought to sell their stock short."

It's difficult to be a CEO, it's difficult to be a leader without a point of view. Frankly, it's difficult to be a manager without one. You can't step out and expect people to follow you unless you have a point of view and can articulate the benefits of it.

When Doug Ivester became CFO "it was quickly apparent to me that I was in the mode of selling something. Selling an idea. So my communication had to move from being purely the facts and figures to the facts and figures plus a point of view about what those meant to my listeners."

My guess is that many, many people have a very difficult time getting to the position of presenting a point of view. I think what leaders have to understand is that points of view are expected of them. Organizations run on individuals having points of view and selling them for the collective benefit.

But expressing a point of view is not something only leaders at the top need if their communication is going to have the honesty and consistency that build trust. It's important to have that kind of communication even with those above you in the organizational structure. Charlie Frenette believes that "it's important to make sure that I've got good, open communication with my boss on a range of subjects. And that if I disagree with something, I am able to express that disagreement and explain my point of view."

This two-part process of determining your point of view and then expressing it is, as Doug Ivester suggests, important to the success of an organization, and particularly important to the effective functioning of teams. When people are encouraged and feel free to express where they're coming from on an issue, the resulting decision is likely to be a better one. Both Dick Measelle and Charlie Frenette have experienced this. "I almost always have my view changed somewhat when I've involved other people," says Dick. "Always the group solution is better than any individual's solution."

And Charlie experiences a similar result from expressing his view honestly and directly to his boss: "We've often come to alternative solutions that were different from what either one of us had originally thought we wanted—solutions that were more powerful as a result of the communication and dialogue that took place."

So in this phase of the journey you're developing more honest and open communication—giving people a clearer, more consistent picture of what you believe and why you believe it. This requires you to do some rigorous self-examination and questioning to develop that point of view, and then to take some risk, which will obviously vary depending on the context, in expressing it. But this gives you only half of the equation. Charlie and Dick touched on the other half: being open to changing your point of view as a result of listening to others. Without good listening skills, this Magic Wand picture will never become reality.

Roberto Goizueta, the chairman of Coca-Cola, puts it quite simply: "In a large corporation, the listening is as important as the talking." Some people develop good listening skills early in life and continue to use them throughout their careers. Harry Caulfield attributes his ability to listen to his early training as a physician:

> *I think that early on, as a practicing cardiologist, it was most important that I listened correctly. There's an old saying in medicine, "Listen to the patient. He or she will tell you the diagnosis." Eighty percent of all diagnoses are from a good history, and most of that is what the patient tells you. I learned early on that you don't learn anything when you're talking.*

Most of us, however, don't appreciate the importance of listening as early as Harry did. Instead, we reach a point later in our careers when we realize that we need to listen better—not only to get the information to make the best decisions, but also to acknowledge others, their feelings and their ideas. It's an extension of seeing the other that was a part of the previous stage. Then you were attempting to see your listeners to get a sense of their response to your message, to get a reading on their buy-in or lack of it to your objective. In this stage, however, awareness of the other goes deeper—and closer to the connection. You see the other because people want to be seen ... heard ... acknowledged. The communicator who cannot do this will never establish the atmosphere of trust that long-term success depends on.

At this level, you're listening for context, not for information—for the feelings and attitudes behind the words. It's nonjudgmental. This kind of listening gives you a deeper, fuller awareness of others, but it also gives them the feeling that you're really with them and that they have truly been heard. This is a deeper level of listening, very important to acknowledgment, and essential to establishing a real connection with another person. It's something Charlie Frenette didn't pay much attention to until recently. His success had been built on his energy and drive and on having the answers himself. It wasn't easy to accept input from others and to take the time to acknowledge it:

> I've got a long way to go on my listening skills. I've found that I don't listen very well and I certainly don't listen empathically. I don't really take the time to understand what's behind what people are saying to me. What I'm learning now is that the harder I listen, the better the communication is. It's far more important for me to listen than for me to go tell

*somebody what to do or get on my soapbox
and say what I think is important.*

Charlie's comment underlines how important it is to balance the expression of your point of view with good listening.

Charlie is one example of a person who reaches a point in his career where he must develop skills that he doesn't have. But even those who, like Harry Caulfield, already have good listening skills, may find as they rise in the organization that they can no longer take those skills for granted. Dick Measelle believes that "the more experience you have the more you have to force yourself to listen."

I've seen, even in our own organization, that the more time a person spends in a responsibility, the harder it is for him to listen because he's been through all this before. And so the nuances of each manifestation of the problem, as it comes in a different code and a different way, are skipped and he just fast-forwards to the conclusion. This is where you really need to force yourself to listen.

Many times, when leaders are in place a long time, their listening skills atrophy, and they end up hurting themselves, sometimes fatally. Their poor listening skills end up breaking down the whole team atmosphere.

I think that Dick's warning should be a reminder never to stop looking in the Mirror. Because at any point in the journey, as a result of new pressures or different circumstances, you find that skills you felt you had already mastered are slipping. There are times in every golf or tennis pro's career when he or she goes back to the basics, reviewing the mechanics of the swing or the serve.

I'd like to end the discussion of this Magic Wand picture with a story that illustrates both the aspects I've been discussing: expressing a point of view and good listening to others. Roberto Goizueta recalls one of his first big decisions after becoming chairman in 1981: a significant financial investment in the Philippines. John Hunter, who is now executive vice-president at Coke, was managing the business in the Philippines at the time and was recommending the investment. Here's how Roberto made his decision:

> I listened to the unspoken word. I wanted to see the degree of conviction he had in bringing forward that recommendation. Young Hunter really fought for that thing; so I knew that, by God, he was going to stake his name on it and work his tail off to be sure it was a successful endeavor.
>
> I want somebody to look me in the eye and say, "I want this because . . ." I want to see if he's going to be willing to fight. If he has that degree of conviction, if he really shows that he believes in and cares about it, my approach is usually to let him do it.

So John Hunter, by honestly and passionately sharing his point of view with his chairman, was able to accomplish an important business goal; and Roberto made his decision to support John not just by listening to the words, but by listening to what was behind the words. He felt that what he got from that kind of listening was at least as important as the logic or the reasons. In this incident, I believe, we have an example of mutual trust at work, as a result of the honest expression of a point of view and sensitive listening to that view.

I want to emphasize here the "feelings" dimension, both in expressing your own point of view and in listening to others. Neither is just an intellectual activity. John Hunter wasn't only sharing his ideas and his logic with Roberto; he was sharing his passion. And Roberto wasn't just listening for the logic; he was listening for the degree and kind of feeling John was expressing. You won't make any progress in your communication in this stage of the journey unless you begin to develop a willingness to share your own feelings and deal with the feelings of others.

By this point in your communication journey, you've turned a number of Magic Wand pictures into Mirrors. You've developed basic delivery skills that give you a solid foundation of confidence and comfort —and that help others see you as someone with authority and commitment. You know how to plan your communication with a clear focus and a targeted message. You have a greater awareness of others, not only how they're responding to you and your message, but also what they're thinking and feeling. The open and direct way you're beginning to communicate helps to create an atmosphere of trust among your team, your clients, with your boss and subordinates. You're expressing more of yourself in your communication, and you feel more connected to others. Where do you go from here? What's next on the journey?

MAGIC WAND PICTURE #4: LEADING

It's almost a commonplace today that "vision" is the most important responsibility of leadership, whether business or political. But few people really understand all that this responsibility entails. I believe, at least in terms of the communication dimension, that no leader can successfully define a vision and motivate others to share it unless he has first mastered all the skills I've already discussed. To help him define the vision he'll need content skills—the ability to develop a clear, single objective and to articulate that objective in terms of the benefits to and values of his listeners. And he'll need delivery skills to help him motivate others in the organization to make the vision their own—a style that shows he owns the vision himself and that he's personally committed to it. He'll need, too, the trust that honest, open and consistent communication has established if others are going to believe that the vision isn't just pie in the sky. And he'll need the ability to listen to and involve other people on the team if he's going to get the kind of sustained effort it will take to turn that vision into a reality.

The level may be higher, and the number and variety of your constituencies greater, but everything you've learned on your communication journey has prepared you for this leadership moment and given you the foundation necessary to take the next step. That next step is a new, deeper level of self-expression because what you're expressing now isn't just a position or a point of view, or your reasons and your thought process. You're revealing more of yourself as a person, and are willing to be vulnerable in front of those you lead. Dick Measelle describes it as the leader "giving an insight into his soul." It's at this point in the journey where reaching out for the connection with others is actually done by expressing more of yourself. The reaching out and the reaching in have become one.

Dick himself is very clear on the necessity to share yourself if you are going to meet your leadership responsibilities:

> *What I've found is that you have to open up, you have to be prepared to share vulnerabilities, to share your own human weaknesses if you're going to develop a true connection with the other person. It's the alpha of communication: that is, you can't really communicate with people on a gut level unless you're willing to invest your own humanity, your own package of strengths and weaknesses and vulnerabilities and fears in the interaction.*

Jack Stahl sees a willingness to be vulnerable as an important part of his effectiveness as a leader:

> *Vulnerability is extremely important. Your group needs to see you as a human being,*

somebody who has the same insecurities they do. It's important that people know that you're struggling with the same things they're struggling with.

Then, though they see you're in a different position or doing a different job or making more money, they're more likely to believe that you can understand and value them. So they're more willing to take a bit of a risk for this person and for this vision.

At his most recent executive meeting, where 250 of the key executives of Cox Enterprises gathered, Chairman Jim Kennedy knew he had to bring more than just his ideas:

I needed to tell them what I wanted in the future, what I expected, some of my dreams and aspirations, and some of the concerns of management—of mine and our family's. Those were feelings as much as anything else; so I let my feelings out. I didn't force them, I just didn't mask them. I felt that was the right, the honest thing to do.

This is the goal that Jim is currently focused on: "letting the emotions you feel come through, because that's an important part of who you are and what you do."

These leaders understand that it isn't just the content or the benefits of the vision that inspire people to commit to it; the personal connection they feel with the leader is a powerful force that will move them toward the vision. And the leader makes this connection not just by seeing them, listening to them, acknowledging them, supporting them; at this level he makes it, almost paradoxically, by letting them see more of him.

I want to emphasize again what I said earlier about the stages of the journey not being absolutely linear—that later stages both build on and often revisit earlier stages. Risking vulnerability in your communication comes only after you've developed a certain degree of comfort, when you're confident that you are in control of your own communication, what you say and how you say it. This is why the earlier stages of the journey, building up your confidence and self-awareness, are so important.

But the experience of being vulnerable, of opening up, can often cause you to rethink an earlier goal and see it, now, from a different perspective. This is what Amy White did. As you may remember, her initial Magic Wand picture was to be more in control of her communication situations. Later, as she began to be more open about her own feelings, she saw that goal somewhat differently:

> *People are treating me and seeing me as much more approachable than they did in the past. They see me as more real. As I reflected on the reasons for this change, I decided that I had had an obsession with perfectionism. From the outside I had to appear to be perfect and under control. I think as a result I didn't appear willing to accept imperfection in any-*

body else and that was part of what made me
seem unapproachable.

So in this later stage Amy deepens her understanding
of the entire journey. Now she's ready to let go and
let more of herself out, imperfections included. And
she sees that at the beginning of her journey she was
partly motivated from a need that, ultimately, could
have prevented her from expressing more of herself
and connecting with others.

THE LEADER AS MODEL

One other aspect of communication is new, or at least
gets a new emphasis, in this stage of the journey. And
that's the issue of modeling. The leader is aware that
he bears a significant responsibility for the communication culture of the organization. People are watch-
ing him, learning from him, modeling him. This adds
an extra dimension to all his communication—because at some level all his communication is "about"
communication, no matter what the specific subject
or listener. This is both a responsibility and an opportunity.

You realize that the way you communicate is
itself sending important messages to your people; so
you take care to define the environment in which that
communication occurs. In other words, you actually
call attention to your communication behavior so
that people can learn from it. Remember the executive who mentioned the video camera in the back of
the meeting room. She was modeling to her people

her own commitment to communication development. Without the combination of vulnerability and self-confidence that I've discussed, she wouldn't have been able to do it.

Let's look at a more complex example. I've emphasized that a leader is expected to have a clear point of view and to be able to state it honestly. But there are times when his view isn't yet formed and he's in a consultative, exploratory mode. When he's communicating in this mode, it's important for him to acknowledge that, not only because he models that mode for his team, but also because otherwise those around him will waste energy trying to figure out what his point of view really is. Frank Cella discovered the importance of naming his communication mode, of stating where he is in his own process:

> I was thirty-five when I got my first position with a big title, vice-president of sales and marketing and many things in between. And I learned something new: that I do my best thinking in groups. I'm not the type to go off in a corner and think about things myself and then come back for contributions. I feel like I do my best thinking within the give and take of group discussion, when I'm able to think out loud with people. I can crystallize my thoughts better and get feedback on them.

This insight was obviously valuable for Frank. But as he continued to rise in the organization he found that his position had a negative impact on the value of this small-group communication for him:

I began to discover that thinking out loud was very dangerous. Everybody thought I was pronouncing because of my title. So if I expressed an opinion here or an opinion there, that was immediately taken as the boss's opinion and that's the way it's going to be. And I only realized that over time. I didn't know it was happening at first. I thought everybody just loved my thinking!

Frank didn't give up small-group brainstorming, since he didn't want to deprive himself of a communication situation that helped him do his job, and bring out the best of himself. What he did do, however, was to define explicitly the communication environment:

I started telling people, "Now, look, I want to think out loud here with you. You've got to allow me to do that. Please give me that room." Sometimes it worked, sometimes it didn't. But at least I was conscious that I had to set it up better than I had if it was going to work at all.

Frank's example shows something very important: that modeling communication behavior for a leader doesn't have to be constraining, imposing a carefulness on what he says and how he says it. Sometimes that will be the case; he can rarely afford to be careless or casual with what he says and how he says it. But it's just as likely to free the leader up to continue to learn and develop himself, because he can model in his communication the openness to learning and change so important to an individual's growth and a company's success. Charlie Frenette struggled with what were, in effect, two images of a leader, one that limited and one that liberated him:

One of the most difficult things I had to deal with was the recognition that I didn't have to be perfect in order to be a good leader. I had some real internal struggle as I was trying to learn new things myself. I kept thinking, "In my capacity or in my position I'm supposed to know that." It wasn't easy to make myself vulnerable and be willing to say to myself and to other people, "I don't understand that" or "I need to know more about that."

So when you start talking about modeling the behavior, I think you've got to have a fairly high level of self-confidence and be willing to take some personal risk yourself to learn the behaviors that you're trying to model. You can't fake it—people will see it. Then they'll decide that you're trying to do something to the organization, not lead the organization to where you're trying to go. And when that happens, you've lost them.

Like Frank, in order for him to continue to grow himself and to model for others, Charlie "went public" with his own process by making it an explicit subject of his communication:

We were putting in place in Fountain a team management system. Part of that whole en-

deavor required a set of competencies—team leadership, team membership, problem-solving abilities, those kinds of things. It wasn't easy for me to get up in front of my group and practice some skills that I wasn't very proficient at myself. But I believed that I had to do it, both because it would demonstrate that I believed it was important and expected other people to do it, and because I would learn them more comprehensively myself.

What made it work, I think, is that I staked out the environment. Everyone knew what I was trying to do, because I said to them, "Look, I may screw this thing up. I'm going to try something I haven't done before and let's see how it goes."

As Charlie shows, leaders are not modeling perfect, polished communication. They model best when they "walk their talk"—when they realize that their behavior has to be congruent with their words, and, just as important, that their words *are* behavior. At this point in his journey, the leader is aware that the choices he makes with his own communication impact the whole communication culture of his company. His journey is now linked with the journeys of others.

So THE communication journey has a predictable pattern, in terms of what particular skills and capabilities are developed and when each one becomes the primary focus, a Magic Wand picture. Perhaps the best way to give you an overall view of this pattern is to actually show you a graphic representation of the journey.

THE COMMUNICATION JOURNEY

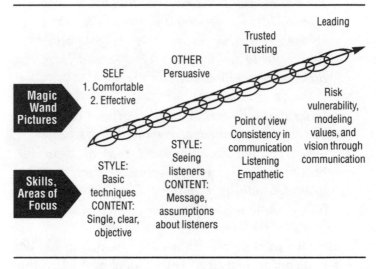

There are a few aspects of the pattern I'd like to emphasize:

- *The Focus:* It usually begins with a focus on yourself, concentrating on those skills that will make you more comfortable, confident, and effective. Then the focus shifts to the other, with an attempt to develop more awareness of the needs and values of the listener. Then, as the journey continues, you're focusing on both areas, going deeper with both your self-awareness and other-awareness. A dynamic relationship begins to develop, where achievements in one area of awareness advance awareness in the other area. In the later stages of the journey, your communication reaches out to the other by reaching in to yourself.

- *The Situations:* The journey often begins because you feel discomfort in front of big groups or large audiences. This is the kind of communication situation that typically surfaces an individual's anxieties about self-presentation. As the journey continues, however, you explore and develop communication skills that help you in smaller group situations—in teams, in small meetings, in one-on-one interactions. In the later stages, especially in the role of the leader of your organization or team, you'll be using both small and large, internal and external communication situations as the settings for your journey.

- *The Timing:* I believe that the full exploration of the communication journey is a lifelong activity. Everyone begins it at a different point in their career and pursues it at a different pace. Everyone has to relearn or readjust at some point what they've already learned. The speed and extent of any one person's progress are obviously affected by internal and external factors. I know that I'm constantly surprised both by people whose commitment moves them to make significant progress in a relatively short time and by people who get stuck for a longer time than I would have expected. There are no rules, no rigid timetables. What isn't a surprise to me is that those who commit to this journey become leaders in their organizations or, if they're already leaders, become more effective in that role.

The most important thing to emphasize is that, although there do seem to be distinct stages in the journey, it is really a continuum. You continue to work on some issues; you revisit others from a new perspective; occasionally you even seem to backslide. Perhaps the best way to make this point is by an example.

When Tim Haas took my Senior Executive Seminar in 1985, he was a very successful vice president of sales. He describes himself then as "one of the top consumer goods sales managers in the country, and recognized as such." He came to the seminar to work on that first stage, Magic Wand picture of more confidence. He knew that being in control was a big issue for him and he wanted to find some ways to loosen up as a communicator without losing that sense of control:

> *I was thought of as someone who gave a very slick presentation. Always in control. Control is a key word when you use my name. I was searching for some additional confidence in my ability to communicate without having to give a memorized or pat presentation.*

Tim made progress on this goal over the next couple of years, but when he was named president of the division something happened. You'll remember his description of his initial lack of confidence being in that position. The pressure and uncertainty of his new responsibilities reawakened his need for control and he went back to memorizing a presentation. He'll never forget the result:

> *It was the first Operating Business Plan I gave as president. All the top bosses of The Coca-Cola Company were there. I wanted to be so perfect in that presentation that I memorized everything I was going to say. Then I stood up and went blank. I totally forgot what I was going to say. I'm not sure what word would describe how I felt. Mortified? Death?—that doesn't seem near as bad. It's an experience I'll remember all my life.*

Under the pressure of a new situation, Tim regressed to an earlier stage of the journey. Or appeared to have regressed. But not really, because, as a result of the self-awareness he had developed from all the previous work on his communication, he was able to deal with that awful experience. He knew where he had gone wrong, understood what would have worked better for him, and then began immediately to apply that learning:

> *I forgot that what I really wanted to say was in my heart and brain and soul, not on a piece of paper. Had I been able to trust myself and go with it, I would have been fine. It really was almost irrelevant what I specifically was going to be saying at the time.*

So what's different now for Tim? "I'm at the stage in my communication ability where I'm speaking a lot more from the heart and listening more to what others have to say. I need a few buzzwords to make sure I stay on track with the thoughts that I want to communicate, but I do a lot less writing out what I need to say—which is pretty significant when you think about where I started, wanting the control."

As Tim's experience shows, you don't advance smoothly from stage to stage, skill to skill. Some lessons have to be relearned, some issues reappear in different forms. But if you're truly committed, you can use everything that happens to you to move yourself forward, even going backward.

IN THE MOMENT

I've used the phrase "moving forward" a lot in my discussion of the journey, and in this chapter and the previous one I've talked about the role of the Magic Wand picture in helping you move forward. But it's very important that you understand the special nature of that movement. People who are committed to the journey aren't racing through the present to get to some goal that's always just beyond their grasp. If they were, they wouldn't make much real progress on their journey at all. It may sound paradoxical, but you move forward on the communication journey not by focusing on the future, but by focusing on the present. The journey is really a movement into the totality of the moment, into a deeper and fuller awareness of the here and now. Let me try to explain this crucial point.

I've said that connection is the ultimate goal of

the journey, connection with self and other. Connection depends on developing more and more awareness of what's going on with you and the others you're communicating with. Each communication situation is a unique event, and contains, potentially, many kinds and many levels of awareness. If you're saying something to me, I can have awareness of your words and their intellectual meaning. I can see you and be aware of what it would be like to be you and be saying those words. I can be aware of the situation or the environment that we're in and how that might be impacting on what you're saying. I can be aware of how I'm feeling and reacting to both your content and your style. If I'm very tuned in I can be aware of my own bias, that is, of the ears I'm listening with or the eyes I'm seeing with.

There are so many degrees and kinds of awareness that you can always learn more about being in the moment. And all you have to learn from and react to is the moment, the particular communication event while it's occurring. If you're only half with me now and half in yesterday, or a quarter in tomorrow, you're not getting all the richness that you can out of this moment with me. And so you're not really advancing as much as you could be on your journey.

The whole purpose or function of your Magic Wand picture is not to pull you out of the moment but to help you make the most of the moment. It focuses you on the particular kind of awareness that's most important for you at a given point in your journey. With this focus you can maximize the learning that the moment holds for you.

So if you're going to be successful in your communication journey, you'll need more than a goal to reach for; you'll need an understanding of and a patience with the process for reaching that goal. If you try to move too fast you'll lose touch with the moment and end up going nowhere at all. Then you'll become frustrated because the goal seems hopelessly out of reach. Amy White clearly understands how patience with process actually accelerates her progress:

> As long as I understand my work on communication as a journey, it's possible for me to grow and get better—and to enjoy the process. It keeps me from constantly judging myself against a standard I can never meet, and creating so much internal interference that I end up defeating myself.

THE GIFT OF THE MIRROR

No one goes through the stages of the journey I've described above in quite the same way. And everyone has periods when they're ready to make a new Magic Wand picture and continue the journey, and other periods when they want to consolidate what they've learned. But one thing is certain about the journey. It takes courage to accept the uncertainty, discomfort, and even pain that come with growth, with always stretching for a new goal.

Doug Ivester is fully aware that some level of discomfort is characteristic of the process:

> One of the things you have to break through is the desire to constantly seek a comfort zone with your communication. Because if you're

seeking a comfort zone, you're going to be at less than your potential. You almost have to switch the paradigm and always be uncomfortable.

But I think it would be wrong only to focus on this aspect of the journey, because I very much believe, after working with people over many years, that there's more pleasure than pain on the journey, more satisfaction than discomfort. The pleasure and satisfaction are the gift of the Mirror, when it shows us that the Magic Wand picture we stretched for has become a reality. We look at ourselves in the Mirror and take pleasure in what we see.

Roy Bostock had that pleasure about six weeks after taking my Senior Executive Seminar. He was meeting in Mexico City with a group of CEOs and creative directors from the Latin American region. He was still very aware of the basic techniques he had learned in the seminar, particularly pausing and seeing one person at a time.

The group was sitting around a big table, and though I didn't change the substance of what I said, I was consciously trying to use the delivery techniques. I told them where I wanted the company to go and what the challenges were.

Roy had set himself a goal for that talk, and feedback afterward from a member of the group was his Mirror: "The guy who runs that region—someone I've worked with for years—came up to me after the meeting and said, 'Wow, I've never seen you that good talking to a group.' It was the delivery, no question about it. I had a much greater impact because of that."

The gift of the Mirror for Roy was pleasure at his accomplishment—and the positive reinforcement that energized him to continue his journey.

In the fall of 1992 Bob Woodson's company was selected for recognition by the state chapter of the Newcomen Society of North America, a nonprofit corporation that studies and recognizes achievement in American business. Bob was making a presentation in acknowledgment of the honor. It was a very important moment for him. The audience included his board of directors, his most important customers and suppliers, the daughter and granddaughter of the company's founder. As Bob remembers, "It was certainly a time when I wanted to project the best of the company and the best of me personally."

My staff and I worked with Bob before that speech, focusing on the techniques and issues that were part of his current Magic Wand picture, particularly the quality of energy and the technique of voice projection. The result?

> It was the first standing ovation I've ever received. The feeling I had was one of elation. I knew I had done well. Friends and customers came up to me saying things like, "Bob, I didn't know you had it in you." I didn't know it either until I tried. It was a great experience.

Elation inside, ovation outside: the gift of the Mirror. Bob, like all the others on the journey, continues not only because he wants to be the best he can be but also because of the highs along the way.

CHAPTER FOUR

SWORD AND SHIELD

———

IN the first stage of the communication journey, when your Magic Wand picture is to be more confident and comfortable, you'll usually focus on some of the basic speaking techniques. These represent the most effective ways of using your "delivery system" —your body and your voice. They are tools you'll use throughout the journey, things you can depend on because they're always in your control. I like to compare these basic techniques to the equipment of heroes in legends and ancient stories. In order to succeed in their quest, they needed the right equipment: the sevenfold shield made for Achilles by Hephaestus, god of fire, or the sword Excalibur mysteriously offered to the young Arthur by the Lady of the Lake. They needed a strong, swift, and steady steed, and they needed to learn how to read the signs on the trail—the stars by night, the tracks through the pathless woods.

Equipping the legendary hero for his quest was an important part of many of these ancient stories. It was important because that equipment represented much more than weaponry and information; it represented the accumulated wisdom of the human community and oftentimes the support of higher powers —if the hero had the discipline and courage to learn how to use them. Whatever the source of this equipment, its power was only potential until the hero released it. The sword and the shield became, not merely external aids in the achievement of the quest, but expressions of the internal character and commitment of the hero who wielded them. They would only work for him when they had truly become a part of him.

That's very much the way I see speaking techniques: they're not some mechanical procedures that work the same way for everybody and make everybody look the same. Instead, like the equipment for the hero's quest, they take commitment to master and they will only really work for you when you make them your own.

THE VALUE OF TECHNIQUES

I consider the techniques essential for your journey for three reasons:

1. They give you a place to start. The techniques take the mystery out of effective spoken communication. As you practice and eventually master such things as breathing, pausing, using your body in a loose and balanced way, you'll feel more secure and in control. You'll begin to "pull your own strings" instead of feeling at the mercy of your listeners. And you'll understand that you have a choice about the kind of image you project to others and the kind of impact you have on them.
2. The techniques give you a place to come back to. When you're having a bad day or when you're under unusual pressure, the techniques give you a foundation you can depend on. Maybe it's an unusual communication situation—your first presentation to the board since your promotion, a media interview right after a plant explosion, or a speech at your best friend's retirement dinner. Whatever the situation that puts you under greater stress, the techniques are a "home base" that will reassure you emotionally and calm you physically.
3. They give you a place to go forward from. With the confidence that only the right equipment or the right skills can give, you'll be more willing to take a next step with your communication. Once you know how to make the choices that will keep you in control, you'll be ready to risk dealing with what's "out there"—the needs and realities of your

listeners. That's the value that Jack Stahl sees in the basic techniques:

It's like anything else. Once you've got the basics and you're comfortable with them, you don't have to spend time worrying about what you're doing or feeling. Instead you can focus more on what's happening with the people that you're communicating with. You can put more energy into figuring out where this group is coming from and where you hope they can be.

That next step may also be revealing more of yourself —what you really think about an issue or why you reacted the way you did. Having the right equipment and the confidence to use it encourages you to move ever closer to the ultimate goal of your communication journey: connecting more with yourself to let more of yourself out, and connecting more with others to let more of them in.

You can compare the use of these basic speaking techniques with techniques in the arts or in sports. We might say, for example, that the most wonderful dance is that which comes from the inner being of the person and seems to express his or her complete involvement in the movement and the music. And yet the art of dance has evolved a body of techniques over the years, whether it's classical or modern, folk or ballroom. And we teach those techniques to beginners because we know that, without this foundation, they'll be limited in how far they can explore the art and how much of themselves they'll be able to express.

Techniques in sports are no different. Sure, there are "natural" athletes, those with extraordinary physical gifts who can hit farther, jump higher, run faster than most of us. But we know that, if they add techniques to this natural ability, they'll achieve greater consistency in their performance and be better able to develop the full potential of their abilities. They'll also have something to go back to when they're in a slump or feeling special pressure—like during the Olympics or the World Series.

THE CHALLENGE OF TECHNIQUES

This may all sound pretty sensible, and even obvious. So much so that you'd think it would be pretty easy for you to learn these basic techniques. But it's not always so easy. Be prepared for physical discomfort. The speaking equivalents of the ancient hero's sword and shield, like the athlete's golf club or tennis racket or the dancer's ballet barre, won't feel comfortable at first. Your body and your voice, comfortable with habits they have developed over many years, will resist the change; your brain will tell you that this or that technique is "unnatural." Here's where you'll find the Mirror of the videotape a very useful tool. You can see for yourself how much more effective these techniques make you look and sound even though you're not yet comfortable using them. This positive image will give you the incentive to overcome that initial discomfort and, eventually, to internalize the techniques and make them your own.

Be prepared, at times, to struggle with more than just physical strangeness as you try to master these techniques. Because often they will ask you for more than a mere change of physical or vocal habit. The way you come across now—what the Mirror shows you—are choices you've made, many of them unconscious, about how you think you "ought" to be or who you "are." These choices are rooted, not only in your body and nervous system, but in your emotions and values.

That's why equipping the hero in legend is so often represented as a psychological, even a spiritual, process. He must learn the craft that the experts have developed over time, but he must also unlearn some things—purify himself in some way to be worthy of the weapon or the secret knowledge. He must get back in touch with his natural self. I believe the same is true of the process of learning some of the key speaking techniques. Yes, they can be explained and understood in terms of the physics of the body or the physiology of the voice. But many of them are things the body would do, and once did, naturally, when we were children. Before the tensions and pressures and prescriptions of the world told us how to be, and tightened us up and shut us down. By learning these techniques and taking them into your own body, you will be, like the hero of old, achieving a discipline and freeing yourself up at the same time. The process will sometimes be easy, sometimes even joyful—but occasionally painful, too. Be prepared. It's part of your journey.

Amy White experienced first the pain of the techniques. She felt they were asking her to be different, and so viewed them as a threat to her individuality rather than a support for it. This feeling was aggravated by the fact that her boss sent her to Speakeasy. Here's how Amy remembers her reaction to her first encounter with speaking techniques in 1977:

> *I think very early I missed the idea. I thought you were trying to teach technique and get me to be something I wasn't, that this was about acting instead of expressing who you are. I also had seen some people who were judged to be good public speakers who were human beings I didn't have a lot of respect for. So I lumped all of it into the category of cosmetic and not real.*

Amy experienced the initial discomfort of the techniques as an incongruity between who she was and what others, particularly her boss, wanted her to be. So she resisted. She never owned them because they always felt external to her.

Many years later and much farther along on her communication journey, Amy has a very different perspective on techniques. Instead of viewing them as some phony mechanical activities that suppress her individuality, she now sees that they can even facilitate greater awareness of herself:

> *Some of the physical techniques like standing and learning to use your voice give you a foundation of confidence and also can get rid of some of the things that may be very distracting to your listeners. But the most important thing to me is what I call the technique of "checking in with yourself." It*

*may be making a conscious decision to check
on your breathing or just check on your feeling about how connected you are with the
people you're talking to. There's tremendous
value in that in all my communications.*

The specific technique that will make the biggest difference—the one piece of equipment most essential
for beginning your journey—will vary from person to
person, and from time to time. This may be clearer to
you if we look at some of the basic techniques to see
how the men and women I've worked with have used
them to be more effective communicators—and in
the process learned more about themselves.

ONE BASIC TECHNIQUE: THE STANCE

Let's look first at the technique of using what I call
the "balanced stance"; this is standing with your
weight evenly distributed on both feet so that your
body is balanced, grounded and slightly forward. The
chest and shoulders are relaxed. This sounds simple,
but when people first try it the strangeness creates
resistance to it, and for reasons that are not merely
physical.

Some women, for example, feel very uncomfortable with their feet apart. Although they "understand" that this position is the most natural way to
support their body's weight, and can see that it looks
fine when other women in the room use it, they nevertheless resist it for themselves. Why? Because claim-
ing more physical space raises concern about what is

feminine, or about how much power they have a right to. For a woman who struggles in this way with the stance, finally internalizing it and making it her own means readjusting her sense of how she should appear to others and accepting her right to the space she needs to be physically solid and balanced.

A lot of men, when they are under pressure, have learned to puff up their chest, pull their shoulders back, and lock their knees. I would describe these as negative choices or techniques. They usually produce two results: the speaker himself doesn't feel comfortable because he's physically tight. And, too, his tight body often sends out a negative message to the listener. It may say, "I'm detached, not really concerned or involved." Or it may be read as arrogance, aloofness. In still other men it comes across as toughness or combativeness.

For someone who has used himself this way for a long time, adopting a more relaxed body and stance can make him feel exposed and vulnerable. His physical defenses are down. As I work with him to have a more relaxed chest and to let his shoulders be easy, he'll usually say something like, "Sandy, I hear what you're asking me to do, but I feel slouched and slumped. I feel soft and weak—and I know this can't look in control."

But they'll usually do it just "as an experiment." Then, when they look at it on the video, they're amazed that what felt like a sloppy posture to them doesn't look that way at all. And they usually see themselves looking more in control and more approachable because they're not trying so hard or tightening so much. Some will even admit that it felt better. But at least the positive image on the video encourages them to keep working on being looser and more physically relaxed until it becomes habitual.

So this one technique, or cluster of techniques, can help you feel better and look more in control. But most people only get there by going through the experience of feeling worse and less in control. The payoff makes the struggle worth it. Worth it also in terms of increased awareness of what is going on both with you and with your listeners. Letting go of physical tension opens up channels of communication, with your body, your mind, your environment. Here's how Jim Fischer, the head of the Technology Services Group of Andersen Consulting, described the effect of some changes in the way he was using his body:

> *I knew that I didn't feel good when I spoke, even though I was very well prepared. I also knew that I wasn't getting the reaction or the results that I wanted. In the seminar I learned that I was blocking out the majority of the environment. First of all I was blocking it out physically in that I wasn't feeling my own body. I couldn't feel what was happening with me—and that actually stopped me from being able to hear the people I was trying to communicate with.*

Jim worked on being more aware of his own body—his feet on the floor, his breathing, and his locked knees. He was totally unaware that his knees were locked until I actually grabbed them and shook them. He was amazed: "That was when I realized that I had been cutting off virtually everything." Beginning to let go of this physical tension wasn't easy. Jim described himself as "literally overwhelmed by the feedback that came from my body as well as the group." But by persevering and internalizing this new "technique," he has changed forever how he feels when he communicates and the results he gets:

> I had been a fairly good performer with my style. But the key to turning my communication into an opportunity to move my listeners and the firm forward was breaking that vicious loop I was in where I was cutting off the feedback. I just wasn't letting myself feel anything, starting with my own body. I mean I could look at you, I could try to establish a connection; but until I adapted what I was saying to what I was feeling it was just a show.

How much people struggle with this technique and how far they go with it is a highly individual matter. Sometimes the change is dramatically quick. I recently worked with a man in a senior position in Asia who was using his body in that all-too-familiar way: puffed-up chest, squeezed-in stomach, pulled-back shoulders. He looked pompous and arrogant—and because of that impression, as well as the sheer physical constraint he was under, he had no audience connection. But this man turned around in a single session, perhaps because he was already uncomfortable with the way he was using his body. (He was practicing what a speech teacher had told him to do years ago!) When he looked at himself on the video-tape trying some different choices with his body, his reaction was immediate: "Well, not only did it feel better, but, God, does it ever look better! So why would I want to do it the other way anymore?"

So he took the technique and ran with it. And very quickly it opened up new possibilities for him with his communication. Because he felt more re-laxed and looked more approachable, he started to get more response from his listeners. Then he started to react to that response, and to enjoy the connection. All of this began with the technique of relaxing the body. And unless this person surprises me, I believe that there will be a drastic change over the next year or two in the way he approaches speaking situations, and over time his listeners will see him as a different person.

ANOTHER BASIC TECHNIQUE: ENERGETIC ARTICULATION

Another very important technique is using your mouth energetically. It's an effective way to commu-nicate your commitment to your message and to the listener's receiving it. As children most of us did this naturally, but because of the control adults either have imposed on them or impose on themselves, many clamp down on their energy—especially around the mouth, which is a major area of control for the body. Think of all the expressions for sup-pressing ourselves that focus on the mouth: "shut up"; "keep a stiff upper lip"; "bite your tongue"; "grit your teeth and do it."

Often, as I coach someone to really open his mouth and "say it like he means it," he'll describe how awful it feels, how exaggerated and out of control. "I feel like a used-car salesman," he might complain. To those of us looking and listening the change is actually rather subtle, but it feels enormous to him precisely because it's occurring at that area of maximum control, the mouth. But when he sees it on the video he'll usually say something like, "Gosh, it's not anywhere near as exaggerated as I thought. And it's definitely more interesting to listen to. It also reflects more of the successful, committed person I am. In fact, I could probably go further with it."

But it still feels uncomfortable, and he'll keep needing the Mirror to reassure him at each step that he doesn't come across as out of control. This is a technique that's easy to describe, but the process of internalizing it is a challenge to many people. Because really to own it and use it can represent a lot more than a mere change of physical habit. It can represent your being willing to share your energy and passion with us. It can represent your being willing to put yourself on the line; your willingness to let us see how much you really care about the subject; your acceptance of the responsibility of getting your message to us. Letting out feelings, energy, and thoughts is both risky and liberating.

So when you work on this technique, you're not only preparing for your journey; you're actually beginning it. In order to master it you may have to deal with attitudes and feelings you've been carrying around for a long time.

I never think about this technique of really putting energy into the mouth without remembering a wonderful but sad little story. A couple of years ago I was working with a group of people in Europe, and among them was a British woman, a highly successful senior executive. Sharon stood up the first day and spoke in a very controlled way, in a flat monotone. She also had a habit of pursing her mouth at the end of every sentence, which projected an uptight, schoolmistress-type image. When she saw the video-tape she described herself as "boring." Then, in her next talk, Sharon spoke about horses, something she was obviously very passionate about. All of us saw that there was much more life and energy in this woman than her usual style was showing, and she also liked it better when she let herself express more of this energy through her mouth and voice. For the rest of the seminar she worked to let more and more of this committed person out.

We were all at dinner together the end of the second day of the seminar, and during the course of the conversation Sharon shared that she was an only child raised in what she described as a "very Victorian" household. One of the things her parents used to say to her was, "Close your mouth or you'll swallow a fly." She realized that her tight, pursed mouth was her response to this internalized, still-powerful injunction from long ago. It was a great insight for her, but listening to her story I felt pain for the damage that a parent can do with a one-sentence statement. For the bright, successful woman in her forties who had stood up to speak to us the first day was still pressing her mouth at the end of every sentence so she wouldn't swallow a fly.

So for Sharon learning a new technique was

much more than changing a physical habit. It was an encounter with a limiting part of her own past. Like the ancient hero, Sharon used the sword and shield as instruments for self-discovery, which literally "opened" her up to new possibilities for her communication.

Still Another Basic Technique: The Pause

Now let's talk about the pause. It's probably the most versatile of all the key techniques in terms of the number of things it allows you to do:

- It gives you time to breathe, exhaling to release tension in your body and inhaling to support your voice.
- It gives you time to think, both about the next point you want to make or about some reaction or response you're seeing in your listeners.
- It gives you time to see your listeners, how they're taking in what you're saying.
- Finally, it gives your listeners time to absorb what you've said.

For all these reasons the pause should be standard issue equipment for your communication journey. With the benefits of a technique being so obvious, you'd think that it would be easy to master. But learning the discipline of the pause is often another challenge because this technique can represent much more than the mere physical act of stopping the flow of your words at selected intervals.

You may resist the pause because you're afraid you'll forget what you want to say next. If the anxiety of the communication situation has tensed up your body, increased your heart rate, and cut down on your breathing, you're likely to feel much less in control of your content. So you'll want to get it out while you can still remember it—and that means not pausing. Taking the pause in this kind of situation is truly an act of courage. Your worst nightmare looms before you. You're afraid you'll go blank, lose your train of thought. You imagine you'll be lost forever in the abyss of the pause. It's difficult to believe at this point that a pause can help you relieve your physical anxiety (by exhaling) and take more secure control of your content. But it can. And if you take the risk and master the pause, you'll have an invaluable resource for your journey. Invaluable not only because of what it can do for you, but because of what it teaches you about taking a risk.

Sometimes mastering the pause requires a change in your conception of a speaking situation, a change in the way you approach it. Many people think that when they're on their feet they're giving a performance. It's almost a monologue: you press this "on" button and continue until you've finished giving out all the stuff you've carefully prepared. But if you can accept that an effective talk is always an interaction —between your listener and yourself—you'll be more likely to pause your performance to check out the listeners and to check in with yourself.

Effective communicators understand that speaking is a matter of thinking and listening, as well as talking. After all, it's the response of your listener that determines whether your message has been received and accepted. Your purpose is not to give out the information but to get a result. The pause can put you in the moment with your listener—checking out whether he or she is getting it. The pause also gives you time to get back with yourself to make changes or adjustments, either to your style or content, to achieve a better connection with your listeners. You'll remember the point I made earlier about using the communication situation itself, while it's in progress, as a Mirror: arriving at that point in your journey when you're able to step back and evaluate on the spot. Well, you'll reach this point sooner if you've mastered the pause.

But changing your conception of speaking from one of performance to interaction or conversation is not always easy. For many people it means letting go of some of their perfectionism, with a deeply ingrained tendency to judge themselves, or to assume others are judging them, by how perfect and polished their communication is. It's always messy when you have to take account of others and let them contribute. It's always going to be a bit rough when you have to react on the spot, and respond to what's happening right now. But the difference in the impact you'll have and the connection you'll get is enormous. And it begins with the pause; it gives you essential time to get in touch with yourself and your listeners.

So here, too, mastering the pause means much more than learning a technique. It means moving from a perfect, polished performance model for your communication to an interactive, conversational model. That shift is not easy, but no real progress on the journey is possible without making it.

There can be still another reason for resisting the pause. In some regions and cultures, and in some companies and organizations, "fast talking" is common. The fast talker who doesn't pause is seen as someone on top of her material. Quick mind, quick mouth. It becomes an index of intelligence. The last thing you want to be in a fast-paced, quick-response world is slow.

Pausing in an environment like this feels very risky. You worry that people will see you as dumb, and that somebody else will jump in and take control of the discussion. Here again, accepting that there is power in the pause is at first a matter of faith. Taking the pause under such circumstances is an act of courage.

I remember someone from New York in a seminar a few years ago who spoke nonstop. As a result he had no connection with or impact on his listeners. He worked on slowing down and pausing so that he could put some of his energy into an intensity he was sharing with his listeners rather than just into speed. On the last day he said, "I can look at the tape and listen to the tape, and I can see it's much more effective. And I hear the others in the group when they tell me it works better for them as listeners. But, you know, at my bank everyone talks fast." I looked at him and said, "I understand that. The question is, who's listening?"

I can think of a couple of companies where I do a lot of consulting. They're full of bright, fast-thinking, fast-talking people. But the degree of misunderstanding in their communication is amazing. The people are getting out all their ideas and information and much of it is just going past their listeners. They rarely take the time to pause and check out where the listener is and what the results of their communication are. They're more focused on their delivery than on their listener's response. No wonder companies continue to identify communication as the crucial element in so many of their strategic goals, from total quality to customer service!

As these different reasons for resisting the pause illustrate, you may have to sweat to master this technique. You may feel that you're risking a lot more than a second or so of silence. But by committing to the process you'll learn to trust yourself and your listeners more.

There are other important speaking techniques.* But I hope the ones I've discussed here have given you some insight into their value and their significance. If you really want to embark on your own communication journey, they are your essential equipment, your sword and shield. You will begin with them and go forward with them. And just as important, the process of mastering some of them will change you. You'll have greater knowledge of and confidence in yourself. And this, even more than the techniques themselves, will prepare you for the challenges and uncertainties that lie ahead.

If I had to summarize in a single statement what I see as the value of these basic speaking techniques, their true purpose, it would be this: they are not meant to box you in but to free you up, not to provide some polish on the outside, but to release your passion from the inside.

---

* You'll find a complete description of the basic speaking techniques in my book, *Speak and Get Results.*

TECHNIQUES VERSUS TIPS

I'd like to close this chapter with some comments on the idea of speaking "tips," because I see a fundamental difference between them and techniques as I've discussed them here.

Over the years I've been interviewed many times, and at some point, in almost every interview the reporter has asked me for "tips" or "do's and don'ts." I've resisted this request whenever possible because, as you can now appreciate, I don't believe that giving people a general list of tips is very useful. It can even be misleading.

It's misleading first of all because the very word "tips" suggests that it's going to be easy, when in fact you may have to struggle most with the techniques that will mean the most to you, personally, on your communication journey. It's misleading also because the word really turns the techniques into commodities, off-the-rack solutions to everybody's communication problems. But, even though a particular technique may be something that every effective speaker should be using, how each person takes ownership of that technique will be different.

Take breathing, for example. An effective speaker needs an adequate supply of breath. That's a given. But learning to do that can require different choices for different people. For one person it could require not squeezing her stomach so tightly that she simply can't get a deep breath. Another person may have to pause because he's talking so fast he doesn't give himself time to come up for air. Still another person may have to let go of tight, pulled-back shoulders to make breathing physically easier. And any of these people may actually begin to feel more nervous and shaky once their deeper breathing begins to loosen them up, because they associate being in control with being physically tight.

Ultimately, any technique will work for you only if you've fully possessed it and made it your own—when it becomes a way of accessing and expressing who you are and what you believe. That's much more than comfort with a technique, much more than the smooth execution of it. It's a condition of congruency where everything goes together . . . where the listener sees that what the speaker is saying is congruent with how she's saying it, and both the style and the content seem to be an honest expression of who the speaker is.

Maybe that's why I never get tired of helping people work on even the most basic techniques. I'm always looking for how a technique can connect to and open up the whole person. It's not possible to do that in tips in an interview, but it is in a coaching or seminar situation. Frank Cella understood what I was trying to do when we worked together: "You weren't trying to change how I breathed or how I gestured or how I paused. You were trying your best to get me to allow my whole self to come out."

That's what learning the basics of speaking is really all about: taking the techniques in and letting yourself out. These techniques may look at first like standard-issue equipment. But like the sword and shield of the ancient hero, once you've mastered them they will help you unleash the passion and power uniquely your own.

CHAPTER FIVE

BREAKING THE RULES

O NE of the most difficult things I have to do with clients, whether in a seminar or coaching situation, is to convince them that there are no hard-and-fast rules for effective communication. Sure, there are basic techniques, things that will help you look and feel more confident and in control. But there aren't any rights or wrongs when it comes to communication.

This is a difficult idea to get across because most people want rules. The rules give them a sense of security and criteria to measure themselves by. But the only real measure for your communication, I believe, is this: Did you reach your objective? Did you get the result you wanted? And, ultimately, did you make the connection? As you've seen in my discussion of speaking techniques in the previous chapter, I'm not interested in things that box you in, but in things that free you up.

Sooner or later, for everyone who is on a communication journey, there comes a time when a "rule" gets in the way. I'm defining rule very broadly here, as something that you believe is the right or appropriate way for you to communicate. The rule may be some technique that you've always used that's been very effective for you in the past, like standing behind a lectern or addressing individual listeners by their first names. It may be an unwritten rule in your organization, like always having to use transparencies or distribute an outline before a presentation. Or the rule may be a piece of conventional wisdom, such as the importance of being aware of different styles when you communicate across cultures.

Whether it's a rule that's come from your own experience or a rule you've been handed, by a culture, a speaking course, or a boss, at some point it's going to get in your way. It's going to be an obstacle to getting the result you want in a particular communication situation. And even more, it's going to be an obstacle in your progress on your communication journey.

BREAKING YOUR OWN RULE

When I work with clients I don't try to get them to break rules just for the sake of breaking rules. Instead,

I help them focus on their objective, on what they really want in the situation. To define that, and explore the implications of it for their style and content. Through this process they get in touch with their passion. Once this happens, they themselves will know when it's time to break a particular rule that's been important for them. They'll begin to experience that rule as a barrier to their own self-expression and to a connection with others. Then they're ready to risk breaking it.

Charlie Frenette took such a risk. Years ago, when I first worked with him as a national account salesperson, Charlie already had high authority and very high energy. He was always in that "winning" mode. The Magic Wand picture Charlie had then was around different ways of using his energy, so that he could pull his listeners in rather than push them away. If this shift was going to happen, Charlie would have to really see his listeners much better than he usually did. At times Charlie resisted my coaching because he thought I was trying to get him to suppress his energy, which, after all, had made him the successful salesman that he was. But then something happened for Charlie that helped him take a major step forward on his journey.

He had always used a manuscript for his presentations. The manuscript gave him a sense of security, but it also was a way of blocking out the reality of the moment and the presence of his listeners. It disconnected him from them. But there came a moment when he really wanted to make that connection with the group. The Fountain system was going through some pretty tough times:

We were making some fundamental changes inside the organization, including bringing people in from the outside at relatively high levels. We were changing a lot of paradigms and it was really disorienting to people.

We had a big meeting in Nashville, and I had a very important talk to deliver at the end of it. Up to that point my usual approach was to use a manuscript speech. I'd take a lot of time writing and polishing it. I suppose it was a safety net for me—and, yes, I wanted to look good. Well, at this meeting I decided to do it differently. I decided not to write out a speech.

I remember the day before the talk I left the meeting and went for a walk in the park, thinking about those people and what they were going through—and what they needed from me. I sat down at a picnic table with a piece of paper and sketched out some thoughts, worked on it fairly hard. Then I went to a party that night and the next morning gave the talk. And I remember how good I felt delivering it.

I felt good, not because the response was good (though it was), but because I had discovered something very important for myself: that, up to that point, I had been "prepared" with a text but actually unprepared to really open up. I used the manuscript to hide behind. I realized that what those people needed from me,

> *especially at that critical time, was some con-*
> *nection. I had to take off the shell. And, by*
> *definition, when you do that, it's different.*
> *You can take a breath of fresh air. It's much*
> *more personally empowering.*

I still have the videotape of Charlie's speech that day. It shows him, not with less energy or commitment, but channeling that energy in a different, more profound way. He describes it as the difference between pulling the energy out of his gut versus pulling it out of his lungs. I describe it as getting in touch with his feelings and wanting to share them with others. Since that speech Charlie has continued to explore this area. He's learning to share more of himself and to see, and so trust, more in others.

I'd like to make another point about Charlie's story. It's about risk. There's always risk in breaking a rule, whether the rule is one you've set for yourself or one others have imposed on you. But in my experience with clients, the risk doesn't seem all that great because the speaker is so much in touch with his conviction, so sure of his direction, that he can push aside anything that isn't congruent with that. It was a risk for Charlie to give up the polish and the protection represented by that manuscript. But he didn't hesitate, because he knew where he wanted to go and he knew that the manuscript rule wouldn't help him get there.

When Amy White came to my Senior Executive Seminar, years after she had taken our regular seminar, she had a very specific goal in mind: she wanted to succeed in a major speech before 2,000 Fountain division people at a meeting in Hawaii. Her subject was something she very much believed in: the learning organization. She described herself as actually having nightmares at the prospect of speaking to such a large group. But it wasn't just a desire to be comfortable that brought her back to Speakeasy. It was her desire to be inspirational.

As I've already observed, Amy's first visit to Speakeasy, in the evening class in 1977, was not a success. She resisted the experience and, to be honest, I probably pushed her too hard. I was at an earlier stage of my own journey as a coach, and at that time I tended to impose my Magic Wand picture on others: I pushed them toward possibilities I saw for them that they didn't always see for themselves. Later, when she returned for the three-day executive seminar, both Amy and I were in a different place, and she made definite progress. She had come into the course fairly insecure on her feet and using her body in a tight, held-in kind of way. During the three days she developed a greater level of comfort and learned to project her authority. But she wasn't able to convey much energy in the way she used herself physically or to convey any passion around her ideas.

Because Amy was someone I had always believed had a lot to offer to others, I was hopeful that we could take the next step in the Senior Seminar. Taking that next step meant that Amy would have to break a self-imposed rule, one that had been important for her in her career. That rule went something like this: Don't let people see your uncertainty, your imperfections, your feelings. Prove that you can do your job and anybody else's—that's what matters.

"When I started working at Coke I think I was a lot harder on myself than was necessary. There were so few women here in management positions. I couldn't look at somebody and see that it was possible to be who I am and still show what may have been viewed as feminine characteristics."

By the time Amy came to the Senior Seminar, I could see that she was ready to challenge that rule— ready because the very nature of her job had forced her to look at and analyze what really helped others grow, as well as develop her own and other senior managers' coaching skills. In other words, her own journey had brought her to the point of connecting with and expressing her own passion for learning. She began to understand that her rule was a barrier to that expression and a contradiction to her message in the speech.

> The whole idea about being committed to learning means you have to start with the premise that you don't know everything and can't do everything. When I was focusing so much on looking perfect and in control, I wasn't allowing myself to take the risk necessary to learning. And I was certainly not modeling the message I wanted to get across to my listeners.

So she came prepared to take some risk. "I was open to the possibility of putting myself into a situation that I knew would be hard for me and that other people would see as being hard for me. I had finally gotten over the idea of needing a perfect performance."

Amy wanted her content and her style to reflect the openness to learning that her speech was about. To do that, she would have to take the risk of opening more of herself to her listeners—breaking her own rule of not letting others see her uncomfortable, not fully in control, having feelings as well as ideas.

Amy prepared for the risk of the speech itself by taking risks with the speaking assignments in the seminar, bending her rule bit by bit until she was finally ready to break it. She kept telling herself, "If it doesn't work, it's a bad five minutes; it's not the end of the world. But I'm going to keep pushing myself to do what's not easy for me. Otherwise, I'll stay right where I am." An important factor in her progress was her changing perception of her listeners and of me. She began to see the others in the seminar as people to share with and connect with, not as judges; and she began to see me, not as the critic she had experienced in the evening class years before, but as a coach committed to helping her get where she wanted to go.

Amy's last talk in the seminar brought tears to my eyes. I was seeing in front of me a realization of the image I had had of her fifteen years before: a powerful woman allowing her whole being to get involved in her communication—emotionally and physically, as well as intellectually. The videotape of that talk became a Mirror picture to refer back to as she got ready for the big speech in Hawaii.

By the time Amy went to Hawaii, as a result of the seminar and some private rehearsals with me, she had a couple of those Mirror pictures of herself communicating the way she wanted to: confident, in control, yes, but also in touch with her passion and using all of herself to share that passion with her listeners.

Of course, Amy didn't give up all her old concern with control. She obsessed over the content of the speech and worked it and worked it and worked it. Overworked it, to my mind, and then overpracticed it. But I decided that, at this point, I'd let her do it her way. She'd probably made as much change as she could handle at one time.

The night before the speech, in the huge rehearsal room in Hawaii, I was coaching Amy in the presence of lots of other people, including her boss. Her run-through was good—not great, but good. When it was over, her boss came up to her and started giving her feedback that she should work with me some more and go through it another time. I took Amy aside and said, "I know he wants you to be good, but you need to know that I know you are good. You've done all you need to do. Now go get a massage, a great night's sleep, then come in here in the morning and do what you want to do."

I knew that nothing would be gained by another run-through. What was most important for Amy at that point was remembering those Mirror pictures of herself doing it the way she wanted to do it, holding on to that image of what was possible, not exhausting herself in repetitive practice. I knew she'd be okay. And she was.

In the speech itself, Amy shared much more of herself than her old "rule" would have allowed. She opened with a funny comment from her child, and then shared some of her struggles to overcome her discomfort with speaking—something not many executives would do in front of two thousand people. By breaking her own rule, moving beyond it, Amy was able to connect with her listeners in a way that was new for her:

> *I felt that I had gotten my message across, but frankly, I was overwhelmed at the response I got. People came up to me and told me how much they connected with something I'd said or how much they appreciated seeing a woman up there saying what I was saying.*

The impact of this experience for Amy went far beyond just the success of a particular talk. Having broken what had been a very important rule for herself and survived, she was more willing to take the risk of sharing herself, her feelings as well as her ideas, in other communication situations. "It opened everything up. It showed me I could do some things I never thought I could, never would have tried to do. I think in the past I wasn't even willing to admit that I was afraid to try. After the seminar and that talk in Hawaii, I was a lot more comfortable not being perfect and letting other people see that." Her Magic Wand picture now focuses on interpersonal relationships and individual communication; she's committed to honest, open communication that deals with feelings as much as facts. She reports that already people are seeing her as more approachable, and more real.

Hawaii—both her preparation for it and her experience of it—was a milestone in Amy's communication journey. In order to get her message across in an honest and compelling way, she had had to share more of herself than she had ever done before. She took that risk and broke her self-imposed rule because she believed passionately in her message. She was learning something important for herself in the process of preparing and delivering a talk about learning. Every aspect of her communication on the job has been affected by that experience. And, I should add, Amy and I have a greater closeness today as a result. We understand that our changing interaction with each other over the years tells us something important about our own journeys.

The rules that these people broke were self-imposed rules: no one had told Charlie that he should always use a manuscript speech, or Amy that every one of her presentations had to be a perfect performance. These were rules they had developed for themselves to help them cope with and succeed in their communication situations. And they continued to observe those rules until they began to experience them as an obstacle. At some point, what their listeners needed or their message required was something that the rule got in the way of. So they chose congruence and connection—and broke the rule. Ultimately, they were choosing to take another step in their communication journey and move to a new stage in their personal development.

BREAKING COMPANY RULES

But rules come from outside, too. Every company has its own communication culture, that collection of written and unwritten rules that defines who says what to whom, and how. Figuring out these rules is one of the first things a person new to an organization does, since his or her success will depend on following them. Some of the rules are easy, like the reporting structure; the preferred method of communication (voice mail, electronic mail, weekly meetings); the format for more formal communications, such as an annual business plan or a budget review. Other rules are more obscure, because they're unwritten and of uncertain origin, like never talking to the marketing vice president about a certain issue, or always using a red marker on the flip chart.

It's been a constant source of amazement to me over the years, especially working with chief executives and top officers in companies, at how powerful these communication rules can be. This is especially true of speeches and presentations. Men and women who eagerly embrace organizational change, who explore innovative marketing strategies and who supervise exciting new product development, meekly submit to the company "tradition" when they have to get up to speak. That tradition may be represented by an audiovisual staffer who tells them where to stand. It may be represented by a meeting planner who tells them to turn in a copy of their remarks one month in advance for inclusion in a meeting "notebook."

I remember working with a senior vice president new to the organization on his first presentation to the board of directors. Because he was using slides, the AV person had lowered the light in the small boardroom; as a result, it was difficult to see him clearly. I felt that, especially in his first meeting with the board, it was important that he establish some connection with them and that they get a sense of him—something very hard to do in semidarkness. My arguments made sense to him, until he checked with the technician, who assured him that the low-light level was standard procedure for all board presentations using slides. At that point, the vice president surrendered to the "rule."

I accepted that, because I understood, being new, he just wasn't ready to take the risk of doing it differently and breaking a rule. That would come later in his journey. Luckily, in this case, the president, whom I knew, wandered in during one of our rehearsals. When I explained my concerns about the light level to him, he readily agreed that the lights should be brought up. From his perspective and experience, the president simply didn't see the rule.

George Shaheen actually began working with me because he was having trouble adapting to a "rule." He had never been comfortable using a manuscript speech or staying behind a lectern, but this was exactly what the speakers did at the annual partners meeting. If you work for a large company that holds annual meetings you probably have a good idea of the kind of setup: a large audience, a platform that looks like a stage set, spotlights and video magnification for the speakers. The speakers are pretty much confined behind the lectern so that the camera and lights can pick them up. They also speak from manuscripts or TelePrompTers.

This had been the convention established for the partners meeting where George had to speak as the new leader of Andersen Consulting. Although he didn't feel comfortable staying behind a lectern and delivering from a script, as a new leader George wanted to do well at this meeting.

Our first effort was to develop a script that sounded like him, that said things in his way and his language. We were able to come up with one that he was more comfortable with and, consequently, delivered more effectively. We worked this way for a couple of years for the annual meetings, and George was handling the conventions or rules for the occasion pretty well. But then something happened.

George's subject for the next meeting was "mentoring," something he had a lot of feelings about. He wanted to speak from his heart this time, and he was convinced that no writer and no script would work for him. So we focused on developing just an outline of the ideas he wanted to express. When he actually delivered his talk, he only used the lectern as a home base to go back to when he needed to check his outline; otherwise he moved around the stage and toward his audience. The result was that he projected more of himself, both in his content and his style and came across as the leader he wanted to be. The positive feedback he got only reinforced his own feeling that the talk had been successful. The video of his talk matched the Magic Wand picture he'd had for himself.

Here was a case of someone who had adapted his usual, more extemporaneous approach to the rules that a special setting had imposed. He followed those rules for a while, grew comfortable in the setting, and then reached a point when the rules got in his way.

When that happened he broke them, not to be different or difficult, but because the rules didn't fit what he wanted to say and the connection he wanted to have with his listeners.

Encouraged by his experience at this meeting, George made a commitment to more open communication among the partners and with clients. He realized that even in a fast-paced, technology-focused environment, it's essential to deal openly and honestly with the "people" issues—with feelings, attitudes, and values. The firm is already experiencing some positive results from this commitment. Partners are working together more productively, and clients have a greater trust in the business solutions that Andersen Consulting develops for them. Having the courage to break rules continues to play an important part in the firm's efforts to realize its vision.

There are other sources of externally imposed rules besides the company culture. Seminars and books on communication are one source, especially those that emphasize "do's and don'ts." We tend to depend on experts in our society, and speaking experts like me often represent themselves or are misperceived as rule-givers or people with the right answers. I know of one executive, fully engaged in "reinventing" his business, who nevertheless won't allow himself to take more than three steps across a platform because that's what he learned in a speaking course!

BREAKING YOUR CULTURE'S RULES

There are also rules about speaking that our culture or our society gives us. I have a very clear memory of one such rule. Saeed was a man from Pakistan who took a seminar I was conducting in Europe. He was improving steadily during the three days, particularly in the area of being more physically involved and working harder to get his message to his listeners. One thing that he and others in the group were exploring was to get free of the lectern. Saeed liked the progress the videotape was showing him, but he decided to stay behind the lectern for his final talk of the seminar, because, he declared, "in my country nobody says anything important unless he's behind a lectern."

When he saw the tape of his talk, he was disappointed. He didn't feel that he looked and sounded as effective as he had in his earlier talks. I'll always remember the comment he made: "I said that nobody in my country says anything important unless he's behind a lectern—until now!" He left the seminar with a commitment to find a way to break that rule when he got back home. The Mirror pictures he had created in the seminar gave him the courage to break a rule in order to be the speaker he knew he could be.

RULES FOR DIFFERENT CULTURES

A lot of rules are coming out of the development of a global marketplace. Companies are expanding into areas of the world and working with races and cultures that are new and different to them. Recognizing differences in a lot of categories is seen as essential to success. One such category is communication. For example, by now everybody is aware that the Japanese, more "polite" than Americans, are reluctant to say no directly. So people are told to use the indirect approach when communicating with the Japanese. By now there are all sorts of rules for dealing across cultures—about eye contact, degree of formality, physical interaction, forms of address, and idiomatic expressions.

John Hunter, the Australian who is now executive vice president of Coca-Cola, has dealt with many different cultures during his career. He's worked in Japan, Hong Kong, Thailand, and the Philippines. He has his own "golden rule":

> *Listen before you speak. Observe the culture you're in. Understand the ambience in which you're doing business. Discover what the mores are. And learn to work within that environment.*

The essence of all these rules about cross-cultural communication is awareness of the listener. Without awareness you can't have a true connection, whether it's with an individual within your own culture or in a different one.

But I don't believe that you show respect for someone else's culture by giving up or changing who you are. In fact, you're not likely to get a connection with others when they sense that you're suppressing who you really are. That's the conclusion John Hunter has come to:

> *My experience is that people of other cultures like you to know, understand, and respect their culture, but they don't expect you to enact it. In fact they're disappointed when you're not an Ugly Australian from time to time.*

This is another area when you may have to break a "rule" in order to make a connection and be yourself. This is what Don Keough did at one of his first big speaking situations in Japan. This is how he remembers it:

> *I was speaking to a distinguished group of Japanese leaders important to Coca-Cola. On the way to the evening I was given a lot of advice about what was acceptable and what was unacceptable in Japan. You know, they're formal and stiff and so on. I thought, "This is going to be interesting."*

> *One of the Coca-Cola bottlers who was there was a seventy-year-old Japanese woman whom I had met in the United States. I saw her about four rows in front of me as I got up to speak. So I walked off the podium, gave her a kiss on the cheek, and came back and said, "All of my life, I've wanted to kiss a Coca-Cola bottler."*

She got a big kick out of it, and all the Japanese just roared. But it violated every rule that fit in that society except one: it was me who did it. It was a Westerner who cared for them and knew them. What it said was that he wasn't trying to be someone else.

Don describes himself as someone who's spent his life in front of groups of people, and he emphasizes similarities rather than differences: "Yes, there are certain things that will happen in some cultures that won't happen in others. There are many places where there isn't a standing ovation, many places where applause is modest. There are a number of cultural differences, but the simple fact is that people, when it comes to communicating, are all the same. I've seen it all over the world." There's probably no better illustration of the truth of Don's statement than the retirement party those same Japanese bottlers gave him a couple of years later—where they sang "Danny Boy" to this American of Irish descent!

Like Don, I believe more in the similarities among people than the differences when it comes to communication. My belief has been reinforced in working with groups from Bangkok to Oslo, from Madrid to Manila. Sure, there are differences, but there are also differences if you're in the room with ten Americans. They, too, come from different backgrounds, different experiences, and see the world through different eyes. You always have to work to be aware and to see the individual human being you're dealing with. But when you get together in a room and focus on what they really want and relate to them as human beings, I believe that you'll get the connection—and suddenly all those "rules" about cross-cultural communication don't seem so important.

TRUST YOUR INSTINCTS, NOT THE RULES

One of Don Keough's greatest strengths as a communicator is that he trusts his own instincts more than the "rules." I remember, years ago, when I was first coaching senior people at The Coca-Cola Company, I asked Don how he thought a couple of them needed to come across at an important meeting I was coaching them for. Don looked at me and said, "You trust your gut. Your gut is always right." I was grateful for that comment. Don was holding up a Mirror for me and confirming my progress on my own journey—something that really meant a lot to me, because I was relatively inexperienced in the "rules" of the corporate world at that time and was just starting to give people feedback on the content of their talks as well as their style.

Don is someone who seems always to trust his instinct when he communicates, and as a result he often does things that others would see as violations of some rule or other. One memorable example was a security analysts meeting where Don was presenting along with Jack Stahl. It was Jack's first appearance as the new CFO of the company, and of course he was tense. He wanted to make a good impression, not only in front of the analysts, but also in front of his own president and chairman.

What Don wanted was for those analysts to see

Jack as much as possible as Don himself did—"a capable young man, with a soul and a sense of humor." He wanted this not only because, as a leader, he cared very much about the development of his people, but also because he felt that if the analysts saw Jack this way it would help the company meet the objective of the meeting:

> *Most security analysts, in my view, aren't interested only in this number or that number, or this fact or that fact about the company. They're trying to sense the whole gestalt of the company. Is this management team confident of its ability to confront the future and are they enjoying what they're doing?*

Coming from this clear sense of the meeting's fundamental objective, and his awareness of Jack's tension and how that might impact on the objective, Don chose to introduce his new CFO in a way that hardly fit the rule for presenting a new executive to an important outside constituency. "I wanted in my introduction to let this crowd of people who determine whether or not they're going to buy or recommend our stock see the real Jack Stahl. In order to do that, I decided to surprise Jack and sort of force him to be loose."

Here's what Don did. At the end of his own presentation, he appeared to be fumbling with his notes looking for something. All the while he was talking about Andy Warhol's diaries, which had recently been published. It seemed at first like a time-filler and a digression. Then he "found" the note, which was a comment from one of the diaries, something about a Coke being a Coke, and the queen knows it, the president knows it, and the bum on the street knows it. "Well, speaking of the bum on the street," said Don, "I'd like to introduce you to our new CFO, Jack Stahl."

Not the kind of introduction the rules prescribe. But Don was trusting his instinct and of course it worked for him. As Don remembers, "Jack came on and reacted marvelously and warmly to that fun. And I think the analysts felt, 'Hey, we've got a real guy here.' " Jack knew exactly what Don was doing and was very appreciative. He truly connected with where Jack was at that moment, and by doing that freed Jack up to do his best—and showed the analysts a management team that was confident, spontaneous, together.

I'M NOT saying that rules around communication have no place and that you should break one every chance you get. Some of them do represent a practical wisdom of what tends to work for most people most of the time. And some of them represent safety nets that may have given you confidence and support in the past. But, ultimately, rules belong to the world where people want to play it safe.

I believe that the clearer you are about what you want in a communication situation and where your listeners are in relation to that, the better you'll be able to decide if a rule will help you or get in the way. Is it congruent with what you're saying and how you need to say it? Will it help you express your commitment and passion? Will it facilitate connection with your listeners? As you proceed further on your communication journey, getting more and more confident in yourself, you'll begin to trust your instinct more and the rules less. You'll let go of some of the rules you've imposed on yourself, and challenge the ones others try to impose on you. Playing it safe won't seem so important anymore.

CHAPTER SIX

LEADERSHIP

T HROUGHOUT this book I've made a lot of comments about leaders and leadership. But I wanted to devote an entire chapter to this important subject, for three reasons.

First, because the communication journey often takes people to leadership positions. During my years of helping clients on their journey, I've had the pleasure of seeing many of them attain such positions, and I've witnessed the time and energy they spend figuring out how to be the leader their organization needs and they themselves want to be. They've all come at it in a different way, some from the head, some from the gut; some have found it easy, some have struggled. But they all work for the balance between doing what's right for the organization and the people in it, and not giving up who they are.

Second, my own journey has brought me to a place where I'm working more with leaders—helping them use their communication to move their organizations forward. I started my career helping people on their style in large group situations; then, as I worked with the actual content of talks, I found myself getting more involved in the messages that businesspeople send out to their listeners, both inside and outside their organizations. I'm now working more with leaders inside their companies, developing communication plans to implement and support their business goals and helping their teams communicate more effectively. This work has pulled together and crystallized for me a lot of my ideas about leadership.

The third reason for this chapter on leadership is you, the reader of this book. I think that you want to know more about it. My guess is that, if you picked up this book at all, and especially if you've stuck with it to this point, you're somebody who either is already in a leadership role or aspires to one. You're interested, even eager, for anything you can learn about how to be a more effective leader. And I don't necessarily mean only a leader at the top of an organization —the chairman, CEO, or senior officer. Leaders can be found—and are needed—at every level. Whatever your level or function, there's bound to be a need for leadership to accomplish your objectives. Maybe you want that leadership to come from you. So I'm focusing on leadership in a separate chapter near the end because all the journeys seem to be moving that way —my clients', my own, and yours.

Very early in my work with people on their speaking style, I began to notice that the speakers who were really effective, although they certainly came across as unique individuals, nevertheless seemed to have certain qualities in common. As a result of my more recent work with leaders and their teams within organizations, I've come to a similar conclusion about leadership—that effective leaders have some qualities in common. These qualities are what I want to focus on here.

A LEADER HAS PASSION

Leaders have passion and are willing to show it. That passion may come from belief in an idea or a mission or an organization, or from a powerful desire to explore their own talents and capabilities. Whatever the source of this passion, it gives them the courage to say and do what they believe is right and take the consequences. In other words, leaders are willing to put themselves on the line. I don't believe you can play it safe and be a leader. Many times people in organizations have made comments like this to me about some of those in leadership positions: "So-and-so never puts himself on the line, he never takes personal risk." These people aren't really respected. They may have the power and the big titles, but nobody really sees them as leaders.

Don Keough believes that there's a lot of untapped passion in corporate America and that leadership roles belong to those who have the courage to express it:

> *The individual needs to take the risk of demonstrating his passion. The whole concept of a business organization is that it's a risk-taking environment. The people who tend to move through the system are first of all people who are willing to take risks with themselves. Unless you're willing to do that, how are you going to be able to lead the company in risk-taking ventures?*

Because leaders have this passion for something, this inner energy core that they either are in touch with or are working to stay in touch with, they resist doing anything that might suppress it or be contrary to it. Yes, effective leaders are sensitive to the current reality and are willing to make compromises based on that reality, but only to a point. For example, as they go into a key meeting they may know that speaking strongly on an issue might harden resistance, and so they make a conscious choice to hold back at that moment in time. That isn't because they don't have courage, but because a reality check has convinced them that at that point their passion won't get them anywhere. The group just isn't prepared to receive it yet. But, while leaders may hold back at times, they won't give up themselves. Leaders listen, and show respect for other points of view, but they won't allow themselves to be taken in a direction that's different from who they are and where they believe they should go. And if they're in an environment that's constantly asking them to do that, they either work to change the environment or leave for another more congruent with who they are.

I believe that a lot of the emphasis today on consensus and team building can actually discourage leadership, because it may send the message to hold back on your passion in favor of the group process. What sometimes happens with teams, especially in companies where "empowerment" is the new hot button, is that leaders suppress themselves. They go through a mechanical exercise of soliciting others' thoughts, even when they already have made a decision or have a very definite point of view themselves. Of course, there are times when you're in a listening, brainstorming, or information-gathering mode. And it's always important for others to feel heard. But too often leaders are told—usually by people who project on to them their own problems with power and authority—that they should hold back all the time in behalf of the team. As a result, very little of these leaders' communication really expresses their passion, or reveals where they really are. Meetings are calm; everybody appears to be listening, but there's no electricity, no dissonance. None of the energy that sparks creativity, and little of the discomfort that is usually necessary to produce change.

I truly believe that leaders who squelch their own passion do a tremendous disservice not only to themselves, but also to their companies and to the world, because passion is what really creates—passion, deep belief, and the willingness to sacrifice for it. That's what you need to create meaningful change. When leaders take the risk of sharing their passion and their point of view, others are drawn to them. They respect it, even when they don't always agree with it. And they want to be a part of it. How often has the passion of a person you knew gotten you involved in a particular charitable or community activity—even though you didn't initially feel that much excitement about or commitment to the activity itself? Leaders who show their passion have this kind of impact on others. Again and again I've seen how energizing it is to others when the leader doesn't hold back on his passion: rather than intimidating them, it makes them feel freer to express their own passion and to let out their own energy.

Roy Bostock, the chairman of D'Arcy Masius Benton & Bowles, rates the communication skills of most business leaders pretty low, but he has met some exceptions, and one thing that, he believes, makes these leaders exceptional is that "they have passion and are absolutely not afraid to show it. They're willing to share and let people know what they think and feel."

There is an issue here for leaders who have passion—balancing the strength of their passion with awareness and acknowledgment of others. Their growing edge is always in the area of giving space to others to be themselves. When I work with clients in the early stages of their journey I try to help them see they have a right to let their passion out. If they're 50- or 55-year-old executives who have spent most of their careers in a controlled, bureaucratic environment, their first step is to get back in touch with their passion, their energy core. What usually happens is that they get excited about letting that energy out and actually, in letting it out, they may initially squelch others. But I believe that, as they continue on their journey, feeling good about their energy and about being true to themselves, they're able to work for more balance. They can focus more on really seeing others, which is also essential to effective leadership. Because once you feel the power, the joy, and the results that come from freeing yourself up, then, if you're any kind of human being, and especially if you're a leader, you'll want other people to have that feeling. A leader has to find ways to help people have that feeling without giving up who he is.

A Leader Has a Vision

The leader's passion is usually directed toward something he's pictured in his mind, which is what many people today call a "vision." It's like the ultimate Magic Wand picture. It's complete with all the colors and details painted in. If it's a vision for his company, for example, it's not only a picture of how much money the company will be making, but of how that company will look in the marketplace, how it will be positioned, the kind of people who will be working there, how it will feel to work there, and the kinds of clients or customers it will have. It's not just an intellectual exercise for the leader, but something that feels right in his gut. In fact, some leaders have this vision before they've even articulated it for themselves, let alone for others.

Over the years I've watched people make choices for themselves and their business that, taken together, were clearly going in a particular direction, even though they themselves were not consciously aware of it. They were living their vision already, because it was in their gut. The same was true for myself. When I began helping people with their speaking, I had no idea that I was starting a journey, both for them and for me. Yet the way I coached them —encouraging them to stretch their limits, to go deeper with themselves—was connected to my vision for Speakeasy, one which I hadn't yet articulated for myself. Even the kinds of instructors I chose, and the environment I created, I now see were all aligned with where I was going.

Leaders have passion and they have a picture, a picture or vision at some distance from their current reality. They use their passion to move them toward that vision, whether it's something for their company, for themselves, or for some cause. And they're not afraid of the unknown or of obstacles on their way, because the actualizing of the vision is driven from them, by them, from within. So they will feel capable of pulling together whatever help or resources they need to move forward.

But there are also special challenges or issues around the vision for leaders, just as there are around expressing their passion. These challenges have to do with moving their team toward the vision. The leader who's connected to his passion and his vision isn't anxious about who he is and where he's going; but he may be anxious about whether others share this vision. His trust of others is in direct proportion to his belief that they share the vision and have their own passion around it.

The leader is the primary keeper and originator of the vision, but it's her responsibility to help others own it, too, not to impose it. Sometimes teams sign off on a vision but then nothing happens. What I often find, when I work with them, is that the vision is something they haven't fully bought into, in their gut. It's more of a directive than a direction. They can't see the connection between it and what they do every day. This is, most of all, a failure of leadership, specifically of the communication that's essential to effective leadership. The leader hasn't found a way to share her passion and picture with others, so that they can see the connection between that picture and what they do, what they want, what they believe.

A lot of companies and departments spend time and money with some consulting firm going through the intellectual exercise of defining a vision. They may have a plaque on the wall stating the vision or 250 pages on the bookshelf, and everyone is nodding in agreement over it. But nothing's happening. Sometimes the reason for this is that everyone understands the vision differently. They've all agreed to the words but have different meanings for them. For example, I worked with a group recently that had agreed on an "environment of trust" as part of their vision. I asked them what that meant, and their initial response was something like, "Well, Sandy, we all know what that means." But I persisted, and asked each person in the room to say what it would take for him or her to really trust someone. Very soon we had twelve different meanings for the word "trust." Once these differences were on the table, we were able to work through to a definition of trust, to a picture of the environment that everyone could agree on. I've found that people usually can, through discussion, pull together and agree on definitions. But it's the leader's responsibility to ensure that this kind of discussion takes place. He must be sure that the vision is articulated in a way that has value and meaning to those who are expected to help make it a reality.

The communication of leaders who articulate their vision and make the connections for their people focuses on the "why" more than the "what" and "how." This isn't always easy, especially for those who come to their leadership positions through the technical, operational, or financial function. They're experts in the logistics and specifics, so they tend to feel that their communication lacks substance unless they talk about the what and the how. But that's not the right level for a leader's communication, which should always be giving people a reason to move forward, to take the next step. It should be constantly making the connection between whatever the particular issue is and the big picture, the vision. This is the way to release energy in the group and help it move forward.

A LEADER MANAGES THE "GAP"

You could describe the leader's vision as an ultimate Magic Wand picture. But, equally important, effective leaders also have another picture—a Mirror picture of the current reality of the organization and the people in it. This means that they not only have a clear sense of where they want the organization or the group to go, but also of where they're starting from. Because leaders have both these pictures, they're always acutely aware of the "gap" or the distance between them—aware of the gap, but not afraid of it and certainly not discouraged by it. In fact, the very existence of the gap energizes them.

Most people, when they focus on the vision and how far away it is from their current reality, tend to get discouraged. They lose energy. The leader sees the same things they do but isn't discouraged because of a deep belief in the vision. But the specific challenge he or she faces is "managing" that gap, finding ways to move others ever closer to the vision. The leader does this by breaking the large gap into smaller ones and setting goals that, while always moving toward the vision, are also achievable. In this way the leader builds the confidence and releases the energy of the group. It takes considerable skill, and more patience than comes naturally to many leaders. One way an effective leader manages the gap is by finding a balance between success and discomfort.

First, success. Leaders want their team to experience success, because that will build confidence and generate energy and commitment. As I've already suggested in the larger context of the whole communication journey, success—turning that Magic Wand picture into a Mirror reality—energizes you for continuing the journey. A leader instinctively recognizes this and is more concerned to move people forward in a way they can feel good about than to get things exactly "right." So, especially in the early stages, leaders set goals that are based on the current reality and that can be reached fairly quickly. They select strategies that they're reasonably certain can be successfully implemented, and in their communication they choose messages that are targeted on those goals and connected with where the individuals are at that point in time. It's here that leaders draw on their deep awareness of others and use their own passion to release the potential of those they lead. Then, when a specific goal is reached, their communication emphasizes accomplishment and progress.

When the leader defines a goal clearly and carefully, he or she is creating the possibility for the group to experience success, setting expectations and showing what success looks like. Some leaders are so self-directed that they don't feel comfortable laying out expectations for others. As a result, two things happen. The leader is often disappointed, and the team has no measure for success.

It's not just setting manageable expectations in advance that doesn't always come easily to leaders. Some have to be reminded to acknowledge the success after a goal has been reached. They're so full of their passion and excited by their vision that they're likely to focus more on what remains to be done rather than on what has already been accomplished. I remember when I first started working with an executive a few years ago, almost all his speeches were negative, sometimes in rather subtle ways. He so much wanted the organization to move forward that he would say things like, "We've done great, but we're not there yet!" Or, "We've accomplished this, but we've got five more to go." He meant these speeches to be motivating, but their actual effect was exactly the opposite. Now he's careful to focus on what's working and to celebrate the accomplishment of a goal.

But the leader has to strike a balance between, on the one hand, acknowledging success and helping people to feel good about what they've accomplished, and, on the other, creating or maintaining the discomfort necessary to keep people moving. Leaders typically don't think that their mission is to make people comfortable. They think in terms of accomplishing some objective, turning some dream into a reality. Because they're always stretching themselves, they tend to make those around them uncomfortable, some of which is constructive and creative. The art of effective leadership lies in steering between complacency and discouragement.

Another aspect of successfully managing that gap between the Magic Wand and Mirror pictures is the willingness to make trade-offs. Every company today has a whole list of priorities and strategic thrusts. It's not possible to have the best and the most resources engaged on all of them at the same time. Because of the leader's clear picture of both the current reality and the vision, he or she is able to prioritize among these many goals and to shift the priorities as needed—getting the organization focused on the goal that's most essential at any given time. Changes in emphasis that may seem inconsistent to the casual observer or outsider are actually all going in the same direction from the larger perspective of the leader. It is crucial, however, that the leader is able to communicate the priorities and any changes in them to his own people. Otherwise, once again, they'll lose energy and get discouraged.

A LEADER WALKS HIS TALK

One of the most important qualities that characterize leaders is consistency, or "congruence." This consistency is possible only because they stay connected—to their own passion and vision, and to their awareness of where others are. So they're able, almost at a gut level, to make choices and decisions that are consistent with who they are and where they're going, and that are consistent with each other.

And I'm not talking here only about big decisions like where to allocate financial resources or what kind of marketing campaign to run. I'm talking about the leader's entire behavior. A leader understands that her actions communicate even more strongly than her words. So she chooses to behave in a way that expresses the values that are embodied in the vision. How she spends her time, who she hires, the way she answers her phone, even the way the office is decorated. Everything she does is a model for the kind of behavior needed by the organization to make the vision real.

And, as I discussed in the chapter on "The Journey," leaders definitely see their communication as part of their behavior. They know that what they say has to be congruent with what they do, that every time they open their mouths as leaders, every time they listen as leaders, every time they act as leaders, they should be consistent and aligned with the vision. And they expect this to be true not only for themselves, but also for the whole group or company, and particularly for their senior team. The communication and the behavior of every member of the team should reinforce the values of the vision statement. This means that their organization has a communication plan aligned with the vision, and defining the desired behaviors. Effective leaders consider communication too important to be left to the communication department!

So many companies today, especially the larger ones dealing with global issues and worldwide communication, end up focusing on logistics when they put together their communication plans: things like how many newsletters do we do, how do we use Voicemail, and so forth. These things are important, but what is more important is the content of the communication. Have they developed messages that truly energize their people to move toward the vision? Otherwise you've just got a list of 125 different activities and tactics that aren't really connected to anything or going anywhere. True leaders, not just those who happen to occupy leadership positions, understand at a gut level the crucial role that communication plays in moving the organization forward toward the vision. They know that their messages have to be connected to the vision and consistent with each other, whether it's a message for an external constituency like security analysts or customers, or for an internal group like factory workers or account executives. This is the conclusion that Frank Cella has come to:

> *In the past we talked differently internally to*
> *our own people than we talked to the trade,*
> *and probably differently than we talked to*

*headquarters in Europe. We're talking to all of
them the same today. I find it's a great way to
do it. If you can get down to the core of what
you want to communicate—the core of what
you are and where you want to go—then it's
right and appropriate for any constituency
you're dealing with.*

The message each of these audiences receives may
be different—tailored to the specific goal and specific
starting place of each listener—but it's congruent
with all your other messages and it's aligned with the
vision.

A LEADER DOESN'T DELEGATE COMMUNICATION

It should be no surprise to you by this point when I
say that true leaders don't delegate their communication. First of all, they don't delegate their personal
communication. And they don't delegate the development of a communication plan for their department,
division, or company. They insist on being a part of
it. They're only comfortable sharing communication
responsibilities with others to the extent that they
trust that those others have the same vision and have
their own passion around it.

These leaders will show tremendous commitment to and ownership for their personal communication. Many of them have speech writers, corporate
communication officers, highly skilled production
and meeting planning departments. But they don't
let anyone else put words into their mouths.

Coca-Cola Chairman Roberto Goizueta puts it this way: "The chief executive has the ultimate responsibility for what to delegate and to whom. Communication is one thing you can't delegate. You have to set the direction and be sure that other people understand it very clearly."

> *I find that working on my communication, whether written or verbal, helps me clarify my own thinking for myself. For example, I write every letter in our annual report myself. I may be scheduled to give a talk six months from now, but I'm already working on it. I'll carry something around in my briefcase, little bits and pieces, and I'll be in my breakfast room by myself tinkering, usually at about 5:00 or 5:30 in the morning.*

Larry Weinbach, the Arthur Andersen CEO, shares Roberto's belief that a leader has to take responsibility for his own communication. "What you do is set an example in communication. I spend a tremendous amount of time and energy on it. For example, I don't deliver any speech in the form that the speech writer gives it to me."

Leaders not only take responsibility for their personal communication; they also expect others with key management roles to do the same. Here's how Frank Cella expressed his expectation to his team:

> *A couple of years ago I sat down with our executive committee. We were starting a total*

quality initiative, and communication was crucial to the whole effort. I said to the committee that I wanted them to spend 20 percent of their time on communication, and I was going to spend 40 percent of mine. Well, as it turned out, that figure is probably about 80 percent in my case today and moving up to 60 percent in their cases. And this is communication in all its forms. I wanted their focus on communication, not on a new cat food flavor or a new color for the frozen food box.

ARE LEADERS BORN OR MADE?

It's always been one of my core beliefs that effective speakers are made, not born. Because the elements that make communication work are so complex that no one instinctively or naturally possesses them all. And what a speaker needs to be effective at one point in his or her life may not be enough or even appropriate at another.

Is it the same for leaders? I honestly don't know, but I'm not sure it matters. People arrive at leadership positions for all sorts of reasons, ranging from the fact that no one else is available to a general acknowledgment that the person is a natural for the job. But I think it's true to say that most businesspeople don't reach leadership positions primarily on the basis of their communication skills. This is so even in a communications company like Cox Enterprises. Chairman Jim Kennedy admits that "most of us got our jobs, not necessarily because we're great communicators, but because we ran a newspaper well. But we end up having to communicate—and to communicate well."

So whether a leader is made or born is really irrelevant. The reality is that many of the communication skills critical to effective leadership can be learned and improved upon. Where the learning occurs varies for each person, but there's always more to be learned. In other words, even for leaders in top positions, the journey never ends.

THE ULTIMATE CONNECTION

At the beginning of this book I said that connection, with self and other, is the ultimate goal of the communication journey. I don't mean that this is the conscious goal of most people who choose to go on the journey; they're focused more on specific problems and concrete results. But at the deepest level it's all about connection—about exploring and expressing as much of yourself as possible, and about sharing in the reality of others as completely as possible.

I think that leadership comes later in the journey because it pulls together so many aspects of connection. There's first of all your connection with yourself. You're in touch with your passion, and with your vision. You have a strong sense of who you are and what you want, for yourself and for the group or organization you lead. Out of this self-connection come other connections—a congruency or consistency in your thoughts and actions. The way you talk to people, the things you plan, the decisions you make, your individual actions big and small, all are connected to each other and to your passion and your vision.

And you're also connected in a deeper way to others. Tim Haas at Coke Foods observed that one way to tell if you're a leader is to turn around and see if anyone's following you. You can't be effective unless you've found a way to tap into the needs and desires of others, unless you see the vision from their perspective, and help them connect with it in a way that's meaningful to them. And you can't move them toward it successfully unless you truly see their current reality as well, where they're starting from and the obstacles they face.

When the leader and the group have made all these connections, there's an enormous release of energy. The leaders I've worked with never seem to get really tired. Because they're connected to their own passion, their energy core, they always seem to have some extra juice, some additional power that keeps them going. They may experience physical fatigue at times, and occasional disappointment. But they don't get deep-down tired or really discouraged. And when the leader is connected to others, and has helped them make their own connection with the vision, the energy that starts flowing in the group is so strong that nothing in the current reality seems insurmountable to them, and no gap so large that they can't close it.

Out of all these connections, then, comes the energy for transformation, the transformation of people and organizations, the power that comes when all the circuits are connected. This is the role of true leadership: making the connections and generating energy for change. Because you have first of all empowered yourself by releasing your own passion, you're able to help others empower themselves by releasing theirs.

This is the kind of leadership that we need today as never before, both in business and society. It's rare because it takes courage, courage to be who you are and say what you want. Courage to risk. Courage to reach out. The kind of courage it takes to look in the Mirror and to wave the Magic Wand. Those who have it accomplish extraordinary things, for themselves and with others. And they do it with a feeling of joy that only comes when you're true to who you are.

CHAPTER SEVEN

"GOOD ENOUGH—
ISN'T"

T HOSE who commit to the communication journey never really want it to end, because through it
they experience ever deeper connection: with themselves, so that they feel more in touch with their
power and their passion, and with others, who as a
result feel more fully involved and acknowledged.

If I had to choose one motto that would fit them
all, it probably would be, "Good enough—isn't."
That's the attitude that often starts them on the journey, and keeps them on it. They're always stretching
for that next goal.

That motto certainly describes why Jim Kennedy started his journey. Shortly after he became the chairman and CEO of Cox Enterprises, he saw two pictures: one was a Mirror picture held up to him by a consultant he had brought in to evaluate his communication; the other was a Magic Wand picture, not one created by him but one held up to him by someone in his organization.

When Jim assumed his new leadership responsibilities, he knew his communication was critical to his success. Within the organization, his communication was complicated by the fact that his mother and aunt are the two owners of the privately held, $3 billion a year company. "To the majority of the employees I'm communicating not only as the chief executive but as a representative of the family. That's an added responsibility. Obviously, I'm honored to have it, but it also puts more of a burden on me." In addition to the special responsibilities of his internal communication, Jim's external communication included speaking to congressional committees about pending legislation and issues critical to his company's future.

For all these reasons Jim decided to bring in a consultant to evaluate his communication skills, to hold up the Mirror to him. The assessment he got would have satisfied most executives: he was told he was "pretty good." But Jim's reaction was different: "Well, 'pretty good' is like saying you don't sweat much. 'Pretty good' is something I've never been satisfied with."

At about that same time he caught a glimpse of the possibilities for his communication—a Magic Wand picture that he wanted for himself. Here's how he describes that picture:

One of our television station managers, who's also a tremendous communicator, was presenting at a budget meeting during the first year I was president. He was doing just a wonderful job selling what he was doing. But then I took a closer look and said, "You're doing the wrong year; you're doing last year." He had last year's actuals and then the budget for the next year. I thought my interrupting to point this out would devastate him, but he just paused a second, then went on like nothing had happened and did a beautiful presentation of the actual budget we were supposed to be considering.

I thought to myself, "My God, he salvaged an embarrassing, awkward situation. I never could have done it. I would have choked up."

That was a Magic Wand picture for Jim, and it stuck in his mind. It made a sharp contrast to the consultant's "pretty good" evaluation of him. He knew there was more and he wanted it.

So Jim's communication journey began when he went looking for a coach who wasn't impressed with "pretty good" either. Since I had already worked with some of his top people he came to me because he'd been told that I would call it the way I saw it. "That's what I wanted. I compete in sports, and the only coaches I've ever had are the ones who said, 'Okay, that's good, you're improving, but ...'"

These people committed to the journey believe that working on their communication will not only help them to be more successful in their business environment but also to be more of who they are. They are committed to their own "becoming," to bringing out the best that's in them. For them, good enough just isn't.

Tim Haas typifies this attitude when he says:

I think I'm a real good manager and I communicate as a real good manager. For most people, that's probably quite an achievement —more than I ever thought I would achieve. But I want to take it to the next level. I want someone to say about me some day, "He's a real good leader." That's the next level.

The great enemy of those on the journey is getting stuck, staying put. Jim Fischer of Andersen Consulting puts it this way: "You continue to move the bar, to push yourself. Otherwise you become bored and complacent about communication opportunities. Instead, you should use each one to do something you've never done before."

I think that what Jim says here should be the attitude not only of those seeking to advance on their own journey but even more so of anyone who offers to help others along the way. "Good enough—isn't" has to be the motto for any coach who's effective and honest. I'm committed to the idea that you can't really help anyone else move forward if you're not moving forward yourself. You'll be less effective, less credible as a coach, especially in the area of personal growth and development, if you're not growing yourself. You must be a model for others, not in the sense of someone to be imitated or copied, but in the sense of someone committed to the process, someone for whom "good enough—isn't" in your own life. One of the expectations I have for all Speakeasy instructors is that they continue on their own communication journey and with their own personal growth. Only in this way do I believe we can truly give our clients what they need.

SOME MAGIC WAND PICTURES

All the people you've been reading about in this book are moving toward a new goal; each one has a current Magic Wand picture he or she is working to turn into a Mirror reality. Since you've heard so much about these people already, you might be interested in what some of those current goals are.

For Roy Bostock, it's "allowing myself to say what it is I think and feel rather than what it is I think I ought to say."

Frank Cella is working on what he calls "ambivalence." "For most of my career I tried to put issues into black and white terms; I worked hard at eliminating the gray. Today I'm working at increasing the gray, making sure that people understand that almost every situation we deal with includes both black and white."

For Dick Measelle the Magic Wand picture is to focus more on external communication, to help project "a much more public stance for the firm on some of the key issues facing the profession today."

Roberto Goizueta sees expressing more of his feeling as the next step for him: "I tend to be much better communicating facts and information as opposed to communicating a feeling. If I feel strongly that we ought to do something, I'd like to be able to show this emotion in public."

Charlie Frenette is clear on what's the stretch for him: "I am very ineffective relative to where I want to be in asking questions and getting ideas or information out of other people. I haven't been willing to take the time to settle back and let somebody else communicate what's on their mind. I'm active and ready to go to the next subject way too quick." Charlie puts this goal in the general category of "better listening."

For George Shaheen, the challenge is balancing who he is with his leadership role. "I've got to remember that everything I say has a consequence. Sometimes I talk while I'm thinking and sorting things out. That's okay, but at this level people don't always understand that process. I've got to learn how to deal better with an issue in conversation. That's tough for me because I like to jump in and engage."

And, finally, Amy White has set a goal for her "interpersonal relationships and individual professional communication." She's made a commitment to "honest and open communication, dealing with issues. There's so much that happens as a result of miscommunication because there's a lack of straight dialogue and sharing of feelings."

You can see that these represent different goals, but each one relates in some way to going for a deeper connection, with yourself or others.

I want to say something else about all of those goals: I believe that the willingness of these people to share them with you in this book is itself a step forward on their individual communication journeys. Their willingness to expose themselves in this way, to share their thoughts and feelings about their own process, demonstrates the vulnerability that is essential to any real progress on the journey. I've already discussed how important vulnerability is to the leadership stage of the journey; but you can't really move forward at any stage without making yourself vulnerable in some way—first of all, just opening yourself up to see what's in the Mirror. You see and celebrate what's there, but, because for you "good enough—isn't," you're also open to seeing the growth areas, and identifying your next step. My clients' willingness to put their own process down on paper is, to me, eloquent testimony to the commitment they have to their journey. And something that touches me deeply.

MY JOURNEY

Just as my clients have been on their journey, I've been on mine, because "good enough—isn't" for me, too, which my clients sense. I won't settle for pretty good for them or for myself.

And in my journey I've had to face some of the same issues and challenges my clients have. I, too, have blocked awareness of my own body; my communication, too, has been driven by unexamined hidden agendas. I, too, have had to find ways to keep my greatest strength—the energy that gets people's attention and helps me build a business—from becoming a weakness that could interfere with all that I was trying to accomplish, for myself and others.

And I've had to explore my own passion, too. At first, when I had just started my business, I was concerned about my emphasis on getting in touch with your gut and your feelings. I trusted this approach in the classroom and witnessed its positive results; but I wasn't sure how it would work in the corporate world. It made a big difference for me when Don Keough held up that Mirror, and he did it in two ways. First of all by direct feedback, confirming for me the trust that I had in my gut feelings. And second by example, because I saw that he, too, was really using the same approach to lead a highly successful worldwide corporation.

I worked on my issues the same way I encourage my clients to work on theirs. Early on in my teaching I spent many hours working with "body" coaches, people who could help me get more connected to my own body and what it was telling me. I also did some analysis of the hidden agendas in my communication. If someone had said to me the first year I was in business, "Sandy, your hidden agenda is for everyone to take you seriously; you want them to know that you have a right to be in business," I would have flatly rejected it. But five years later and much farther along on my own journey, I was able to acknowledge that this motive was indeed behind my pushing people so hard and using my energy in a more performing than interacting way. I needed to get results and approval from them to prove something to myself.

This work, both physical and mental, on my own self-awareness brought me to a greater comfort with myself. After years of feedback and videotaping and self-questioning, I became confident that my own communication was effective and was ready to focus all my attention on the other. I stopped worrying about how I was doing, and people opened up to me in a way they never had before.

My books have definitely been a part of my journey. Each one represents a next step for me, because I had to make myself vulnerable to accomplish my objective for it. My first book took ideas that I'd used successfully in the classroom and put them out there for everybody to scrutinize—all those communication "experts" in the academic and business worlds. I was nervous about how others would receive those ideas. In my second book, *Speak and Get Results*, I was trying to establish myself, not merely as a "speech" coach who could help people with the delivery of their speeches and presentations, but as a businessperson who understood the communication needs of businesspeople, in both the style and content areas. Would others see me that way?

This book, too, is a next step for me. And it represents perhaps the biggest risk of all. It's the strongest statement of my own beliefs and values that I've ever put on paper. The people I work with know these values and beliefs, but here I'm sharing them with a wider audience, one that doesn't know me, and with whom I have no personal connection. But the courage of those very people I work with, particularly those who have shared their own process so openly for this book, has given me the courage to share my beliefs with you.

My courage had another source, however: my own passion. The passion that comes from my belief in the power of the communication journey. Unlike my other two books, this isn't really a "how to" book. It's a "why" book. Why commit to long-term communication development? By now you know my answer to that question: because there is no more effective instrument for personal and professional growth. This is my belief not just after a few years in the classroom and a few more years in business but after more than two decades of working on myself and with others. It's the fruit of my life's work to this point. Whatever the risk, I had to share the message about the journey with more people—to share it with you.

You probably wouldn't be reading this book if "good enough—isn't" for you, too. I hope that what you've read here has given you a glimpse of the possibilities, maybe even convinced you to put some of your energy for achievement and self-actualization into communication development. That's why I wrote this book. I hope that what I and my clients have said here will inspire you to look in the Mirror, to wave the Magic Wand, and start a journey of your own.

About the Author

SANDY LINVER is the president of Speakeasy Inc., a communication consulting company with offices in Atlanta and San Francisco. Speakeasy helps leaders at all levels reach their full potential through more effective communication—internally, with their colleagues, and externally, with their clients. In addition, the company assists clients to define and implement communication strategy. Speakeasy's mission is to help executives reach their personal and business goals by maximizing their communication power. Clients include The Coca-Cola Company, Andersen Consulting, Arthur Andersen, Motorola, Kaiser Permanente, and UPS.

Internationally recognized as an expert on communication, Sandy Linver works with top executives, conducts special seminars, and facilitates meetings for clients. She is also the author of *Speak Easy* and *Speak and Get Results*.

For more information on courses, books, and tapes, please contact Speakeasy Inc., 3414 Peachtree Road NE, Suite 800, Atlanta, GA 30326; telephone: 404-261-4029; fax: 404-266-1898.